Basic Subtraction Facts to 18

> Turn to each section to find a more detailed skills list.

Table of Contents

What Does This Book Include?

- More than 80 student practice pages that build basic math skills
- A detailed skills list for each section of the book
- Send-home letters informing parents of the skills being targeted and ways to practice these skills
- Timed student checkups
- A reproducible student progress chart
- Awards to celebrate student progress
- Answer keys for easy checking
- Perforated pages for easy removal and filing if desired

What Are the Benefits of This Book?

- Organized for quick and easy use
- Enhances and supports your existing math program
- Offers four to six reproducible practice pages for each basic subtraction skill
- Helps develop mastery of basic facts
- Provides reinforcement for different ability levels
- Includes communication pages that encourage parents' participation in their children's learning of math
- Contains checkups that assess students' subtraction knowledge
- Offers a reproducible chart for documenting student progress
- Aligns with national math standards

©2004 by THE EDUCATION CENTER, INC.
All rights reserved.
ISBN# 1-56234-591-5

D1519075

How to Use This Book
Steps to Success

Choose Skills to Target
Scan the detailed table of contents at the beginning of each section to find just the right skills to target your students' needs.

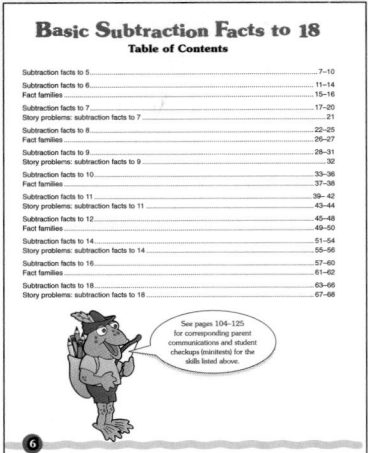

Select Fun Practice Pages
Choose from a variety of fun formats the pages that best match your students' current ability levels.

Fun Formats

Date Skill Completed

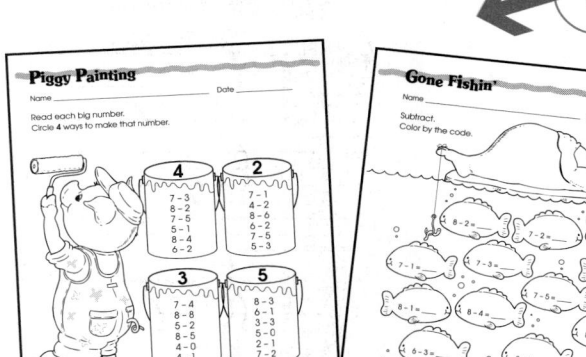

Targeted Skill

Letter to Parents Informing Them of Skill to Review

Communicate With Parents
Recruit parent assistance by locating the appropriate parent letter (pages 104–124), making copies, and sending the letter home.

Facts to Practice

Simple At-Home Activity

Assess Student Understanding

Assess students' progress with student checkups (mini tests) on pages 105–125. Choose Checkup A or Checkup B.

Checkup 4

Name _____ Date _____

A.	5 − 3	4 − 1	7 − 2	8 − 5	6 − 4
B.	7 − 3	4 − 0	7 − 6	8 − 3	6 − 6
C.	8 − 7	6 − 1	5 − 2	7 − 7	8 − 4
D.	6 − 3	5 − 1	8 − 2	8 − 6	7 − 4
E.	4 − 3	3 − 2	2 − 2	5 − 0	4 − 2

Test A: Subtraction facts to 8

Checkup 4

Name _____ Date _____

A.	8 − 0	6 − 2	5 − 4	6 − 0	4 − 2
B.	7 − 1	4 − 3	8 − 5	7 − 5	6 − 5
C.	8 − 7	7 − 0	8 − 1	6 − 3	8 − 4
D.	7 − 3	8 − 8	6 − 2	5 − 5	8 − 6
E.	5 − 3	2 − 0	3 − 2	4 − 1	3 − 3

Test B: Subtraction facts to 8

Two Checkups for Each Skill

Document Progress

Documenting student progress can be as easy as 1, 2, 3! Do the following for each student:
1. Make a copy of the Student Progress Chart (page 103).
2. File the chart in his math portfolio or a class notebook.
3. Record the date each checkup is given, the number of correct answers, and any comments regarding his progress.

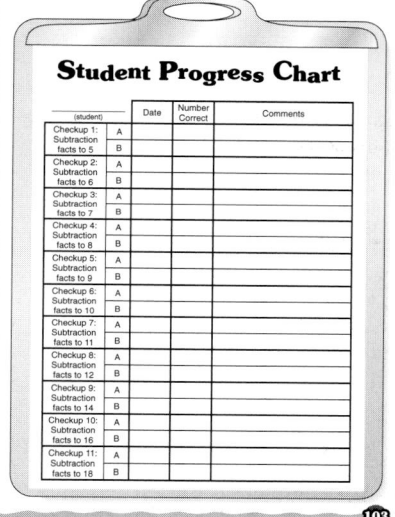

Student Progress Chart

(student)		Date	Number Correct	Comments
Checkup 1: Subtraction facts to 5	A			
	B			
Checkup 2: Subtraction facts to 6	A			
	B			
Checkup 3: Subtraction facts to 7	A			
	B			
Checkup 4: Subtraction facts to 8	A			
	B			
Checkup 5: Subtraction facts to 9	A			
	B			
Checkup 6: Subtraction facts to 10	A			
	B			
Checkup 7: Subtraction facts to 11	A			
	B			
Checkup 8: Subtraction facts to 12	A			
	B			
Checkup 9: Subtraction facts to 14	A			
	B			
Checkup 10: Subtraction facts to 16	A			
	B			
Checkup 11: Subtraction facts to 18	A			
	B			

103

Celebrate!

Celebrate subtraction success using the awards on page 126.

It's a fact!

_____

can subtract!

Teacher

Date

3

Books in the Target Math Success series include

- *Basic Addition Facts to 18*
- *Basic Subtraction Facts to 18*
- *Addition of Larger Numbers*
- *Subtraction of Larger Numbers*
- *Basic Multiplication Facts and More*
- *Basic Division Facts and More*
- *Multiplication of Larger Numbers*
- *Division of Larger Numbers*
- *Fractions*
- *Decimals*

Managing Editor: Kelly Coder
Editor at Large: Diane Badden
Staff Editor: Deborah G. Swider
Copy Editors: Tazmen Carlisle, Amy Kirtley-Hill, Karen L. Mayworth, Kristy Parton, Debbie Shoffner, Cathy Edwards Simrell
Art Coordinator: Pam Crane
Artists: Pam Crane, Theresa Lewis Goode, Clevell Harris, Ivy L. Koonce, Clint Moore, Greg D. Rieves, Rebecca Saunders, Barry Slate, Stuart Smith, Donna K. Teal
The Mailbox® Books.com: Judy P. Wyndham (MANAGER); Jennifer Tipton Bennett (DESIGNER/ARTIST); Karen White (INTERNET COORDINATOR); Paul Fleetwood, Xiaoyun Wu (SYSTEMS)

President, The Mailbox Book Company™: Joseph C. Bucci
Director of Book Planning and Development: Chris Poindexter
Curriculum Director: Karen P. Shelton
Book Development Managers: Cayce Guiliano, Elizabeth H. Lindsay, Thad McLaurin
Editorial Planning: Kimberley Bruck (MANAGER); Debra Liverman, Sharon Murphy, Susan Walker (TEAM LEADERS)
Editorial and Freelance Management: Karen A. Brudnak; Sarah Hamblet, Hope Rodgers (EDITORIAL ASSISTANTS)
Editorial Production: Lisa K. Pitts (TRAFFIC MANAGER); Lynette Dickerson (TYPE SYSTEMS); Mark Rainey (TYPESETTER)
Librarian: Dorothy C. McKinney

www.themailbox.com

Basic Subtraction Facts to 18

Basic Subtraction Facts to 18

Table of Contents

*See pages 104–125 for corresponding parent communications and student checkups (minitests) for these skills.

Home Run Hitters

Name _____   Date _____

Count.
Subtract.
Write the math sentence.

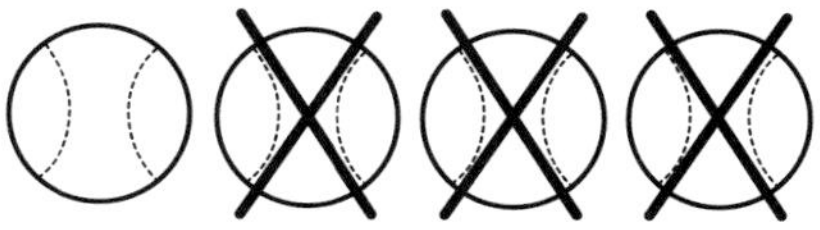

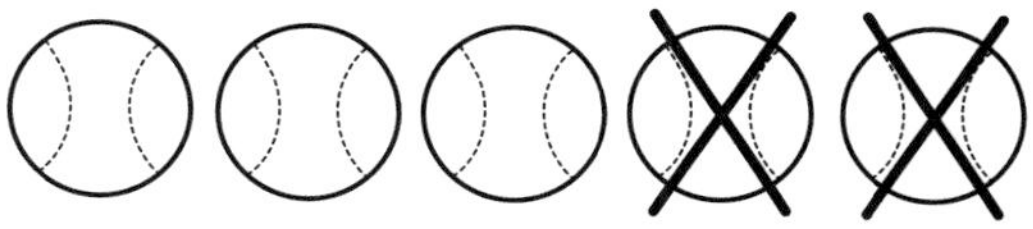

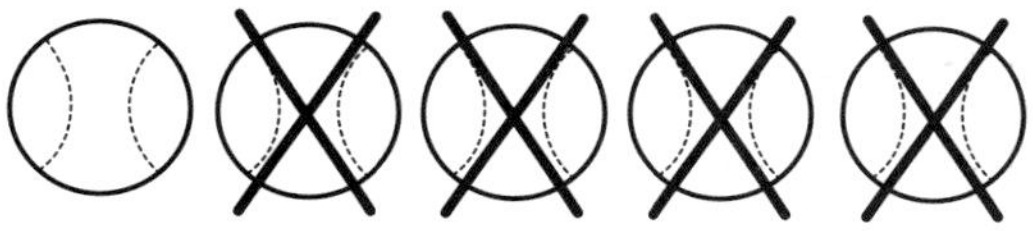

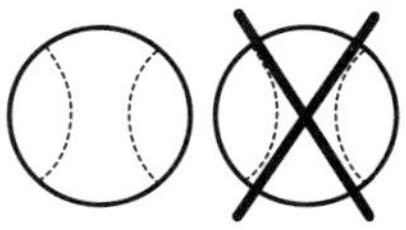

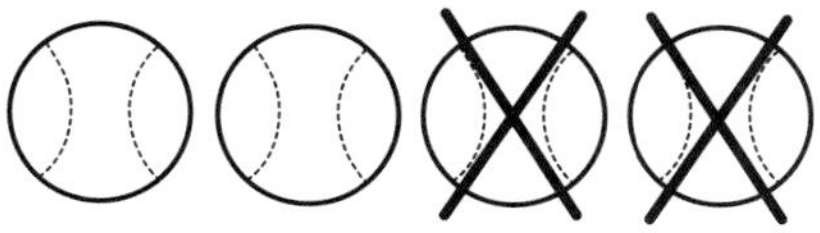

Home	Visitors
5	4

_____ - _____ = _____

_____ - _____ = _____

_____ - _____ = _____

_____ - _____ = _____

_____ - _____ = _____

_____ - _____ = _____

Subtraction facts to 5   7

Camel's Candy Shop

Name _____   Date _____

Count.
Subtract.
Write the math sentence.

_____ - _____ = _____

_____ - _____ = _____

_____ - _____ = _____

_____ - _____ = _____

_____ - _____ = _____

_____ - _____ = _____

_____ - _____ = _____

_____ - _____ = _____

Subtraction facts to 5

Road Crew

Name _____   Date _____

Subtract.
Color by the code.

Color Code
0 or 1—orange
2 or 3—yellow
4 or 5—red

Road Crew

5 – 0 = _____

4 – 1 = _____

3 – 2 = _____

4 – 0 = _____

3 – 1 = _____

2 – 2 = _____

4 – 2 = _____

4 – 3 = _____

2 – 1 = _____

3 – 0 = _____

5 – 1 = _____

5 – 2 = _____

5 – 3 = _____

5 – 5 = _____

2 – 0 = _____

5 – 4 = _____

Doctor on Call

Name _____ Date _____

Subtract.
Help Dr. Ducky find his bag.
If the answer is **3, 4,** or **5,** color the clipboard **brown**.

3 − 3	5 − 4	4 − 2	5 − 1
2 − 1	4 − 0	5 − 2	5 − 0
3 − 0	4 − 1	3 − 2	2 − 2
5 − 1	1 − 0	1 − 1	4 − 0
4 − 1	5 − 2	5 − 0	3 − 0

Golfin' Dolphins

Name _____ Date _____

Count.
Subtract.
Write the math sentence.

_____ − _____ = _____

_____ − _____ = _____

_____ − _____ = _____

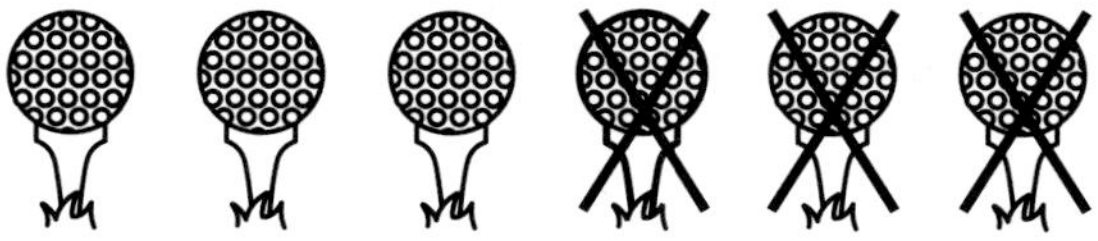

_____ − _____ = _____

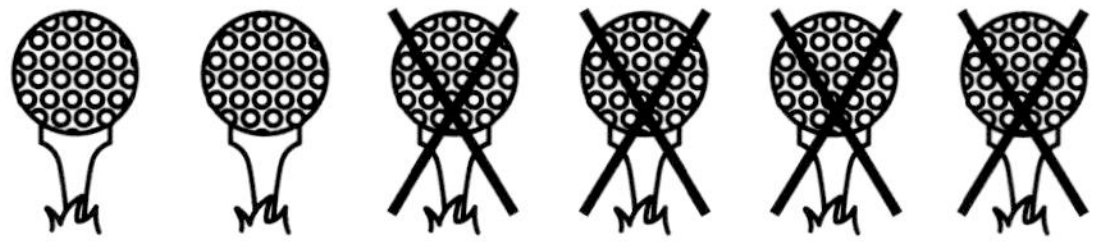

_____ − _____ = _____

_____ − _____ = _____

_____ − _____ = _____

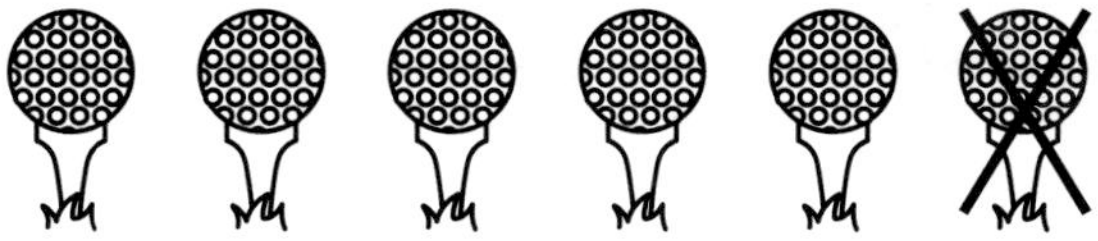

_____ − _____ = _____

Cookie Countdown

Name _____   Date _____

Count.
Cross off cookies to subtract.
Write the answer.

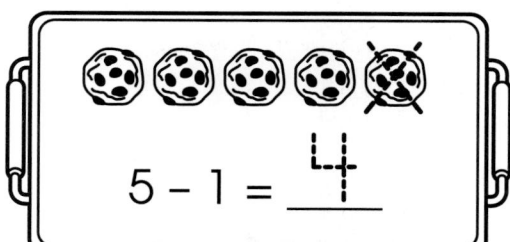

$5 - 1 = $ __4__

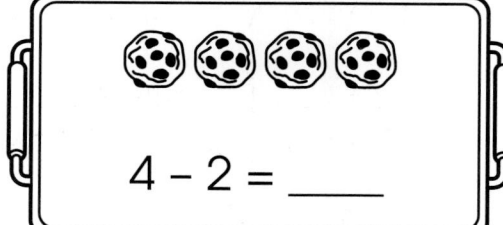

$4 - 2 = $ _____

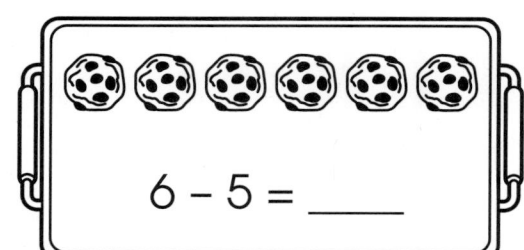

$6 - 5 = $ _____

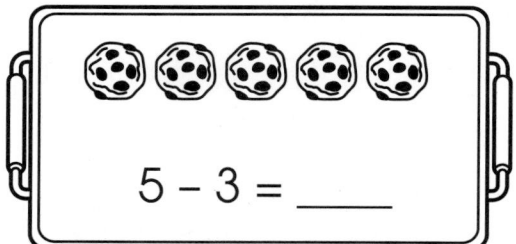

$5 - 3 = $ _____

$2 - 1 = $ _____

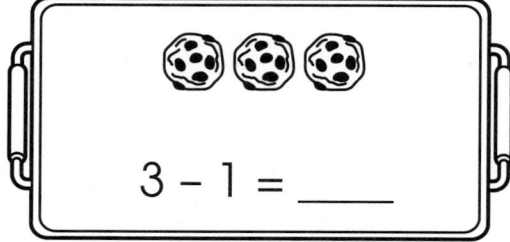

$3 - 1 = $ _____

$6 - 3 = $ _____

$4 - 3 = $ _____

Beach Bound

Name _____ Date _____

Subtract.
Color by the code.

5 – 1 = ____ | 3 – 3 = ____

4 – 2 = ____ | 5 – 2 = ____

5 – 4 = ____ | 6 – 1 = ____

5 – 0 = ____ | 6 – 2 = ____

3 – 2 = ____ | 6 – 3 = ____

6 – 6 = ____ | 6 – 4 = ____

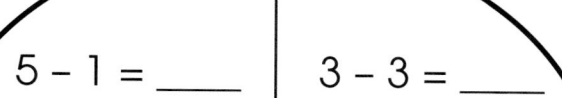

6 – 5 = ____ | 5 – 5 = ____

5 – 3 = ____ | 4 – 0 = ____

4 – 1 = ____ | 6 – 1 = ____

©The Education Center, Inc. • *Target Math Success* • TEC60826 • Key p. 127

Off to School

Name _____ Date _____

Subtract.
Help Freddie Fish find his way to school.
If the answer is **1, 2,** or **3,** color the bubble **blue.**

©The Education Center, Inc. • *Target Math Success* • TEC60826 • Key p. 127

Family Photos

Name _____   Date _____

Add and subtract.

4 − 1 = _____

3 + 1 = _____

4 − 3 = _____

1 + 3 = _____

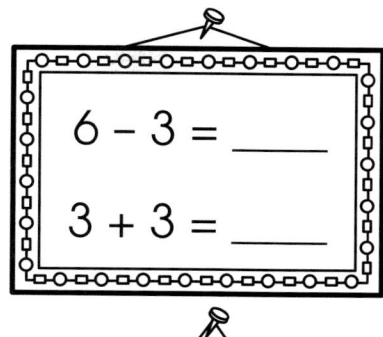

6 − 3 = _____

3 + 3 = _____

6 − 5 = _____

5 + 1 = _____

6 − 1 = _____

1 + 5 = _____

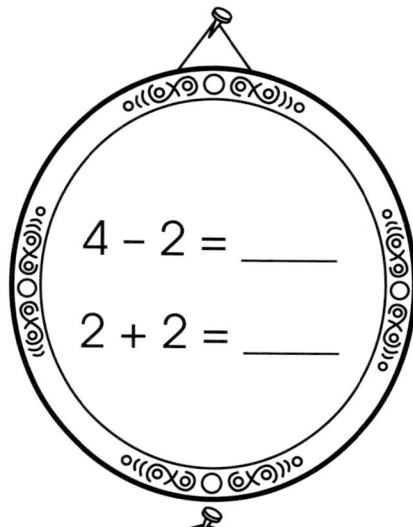

4 − 2 = _____

2 + 2 = _____

7 − 1 = _____

1 + 6 = _____

7 − 6 = _____

6 + 1 = _____

2 − 1 = _____

1 + 1 = _____

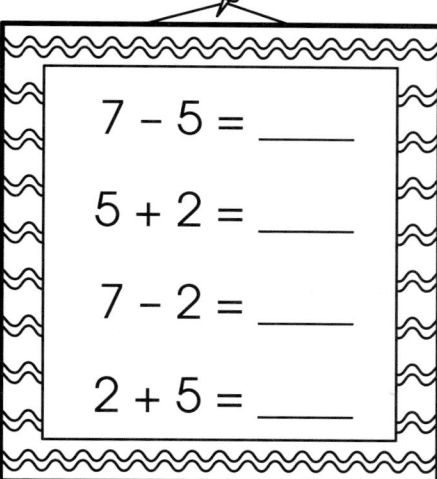

7 − 5 = _____

5 + 2 = _____

7 − 2 = _____

2 + 5 = _____

Wow!

Oh my!

Family "Buzz-ness"

Name _____ Date _____

Add and subtract.
Write the numbers for each fact family on the flowers.

5 − 2 = __3__

2 + 3 = ____

5 − 3 = ____

3 + 2 = ____

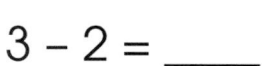

3 − 2 = ____

1 + 2 = ____

3 − 1 = ____

2 + 1 = ____

6 − 2 = ____

2 + 4 = ____

6 − 4 = ____

4 + 2 = ____

5 − 1 = ____

1 + 4 = ____

5 − 4 = ____

4 + 1 = ____

Monkeying Around With Marbles

Name _____ Date _____

Subtract.
Cross off a
matching answer.

6 − 3	5 − 1	6 − 2	6 − 1	3 − 2
4 − 3	7 − 0	7 − 1	5 − 3	7 − 5
7 − 2	6 − 5	7 − 3		
4 − 2	6 − 0	7 − 4		

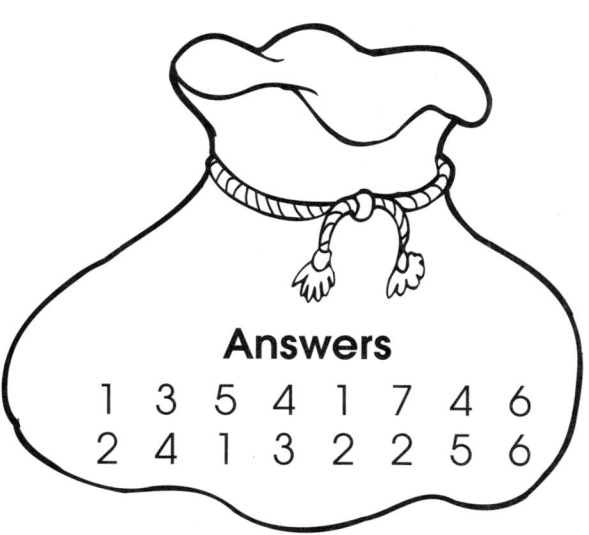

Answers

1 3 5 4 1 7 4 6
2 4 1 3 2 2 5 6

Cheep, Cheep!

Name _____   Date _____

Subtract.
Color by the code.

Color Code
1—orange   2 or 3—yellow
4—green   5—brown
6—red

6 – 0 = _____

3 – 2 = _____

7 – 5 = _____

2 – 1 = _____

6 – 1 = _____   7 – 1 = _____

4 – 1 = _____

5 – 3 = _____   6 – 4 = _____   6 – 0 = _____

6 – 2 = _____

3 – 0 = _____

6 – 3 = _____

7 – 4 = _____

7 – 3 = _____

Subtraction facts to 7

Munch, Munch

Name _____   Date _____

Subtract.
Color by the code.

Color Code
0, 1, or 2—brown   3—green
4—orange   5, 6, or 7—blue

7 − 2 = ____

6 − 0 = ____

6 − 1 = ____

7 − 1 = ____

6 − 2 = ____

5 − 1 = ____

7 − 0 = ____

4 − 0 = ____

6 − 4 = ____

7 − 3 = ____

7 − 7 = ____

7 − 6 = ____

4 − 4 = ____

3 − 1 = ____

7 − 3 = ____

6 − 5 = ____

5 − 4 = ____

4 − 2 = ____

3 − 3 = ____

5 − 5 = ____

6 − 3 = ____

7 − 4 = ____

Time for Bed

Name _____ Date _____

Subtract.

Help Eddie find his toothbrush.

If the answer is **5, 6,** or **7,**
   color the box **green.**

5 − 3	7 − 2	6 − 1	7 − 0	5 − 4
4 − 2	6 − 0	3 − 1	3 − 0	2 − 2
1 − 1	5 − 0	7 − 1	6 − 1	7 − 6
7 − 3	6 − 4	5 − 5	7 − 0	6 − 5
6 − 0	7 − 1	5 − 0	7 − 2	7 − 4

Subtraction facts to 7

Yummy Carrot Patch

Name _____ Date _____

Read.
Write the math sentence.

Bunny plants **4** 🌰.
She takes **2** 🌰 out.
How many 🌰 are left?

_____ − _____ = _____

There are **3** 🥕.
Bunny eats **1** 🥕.
How many 🥕 are left?

_____ − _____ = _____

There are **5** seeds.
Bunny uses **1** seeds.
How many seeds are left?

_____ − _____ = _____

The seed pack has **7** 🌰.
Bunny plants **6** 🌰.
How many 🌰 are left?

_____ − _____ = _____

Bunny has **6** seeds.
Her friend uses **2** seeds.
How many seeds are left?

_____ − _____ = _____

Bunny has **7** 🥕.
She puts **3** 🥕 in a
   lunchbox.
How many 🥕 are left?

_____ − _____ = _____

Piggy Painting

Name _____   Date _____

Read each big number.
Circle **4** ways to make that number.

4
7 – 3
8 – 2
7 – 5
5 – 1
8 – 4
6 – 2

2
7 – 1
4 – 2
8 – 6
6 – 2
7 – 5
5 – 3

3
7 – 4
8 – 8
5 – 2
8 – 5
4 – 0
4 – 1

5
8 – 3
6 – 1
3 – 3
5 – 0
2 – 1
7 – 2

Gone Fishin'

Name _____ Date _____

Subtract.
Color by the code.

8 − 2 = _____

7 − 2 = _____

8 − 0 = _____

7 − 1 = _____

7 − 3 = _____

7 − 4 = _____

7 − 5 = _____

8 − 1 = _____

8 − 4 = _____

8 − 5 = _____

6 − 3 = _____

8 − 3 = _____

4 − 1 = _____

8 − 6 = _____

Color Code
2 or 3—yellow
4 or 5—blue
6, 7, or 8—green

Subtraction facts to 8

Hopping Home

Name _____   Date _____

Subtract.
Help Frog find his home.
If the answer is **4, 5,** or **6,** color the lily pad **green.**

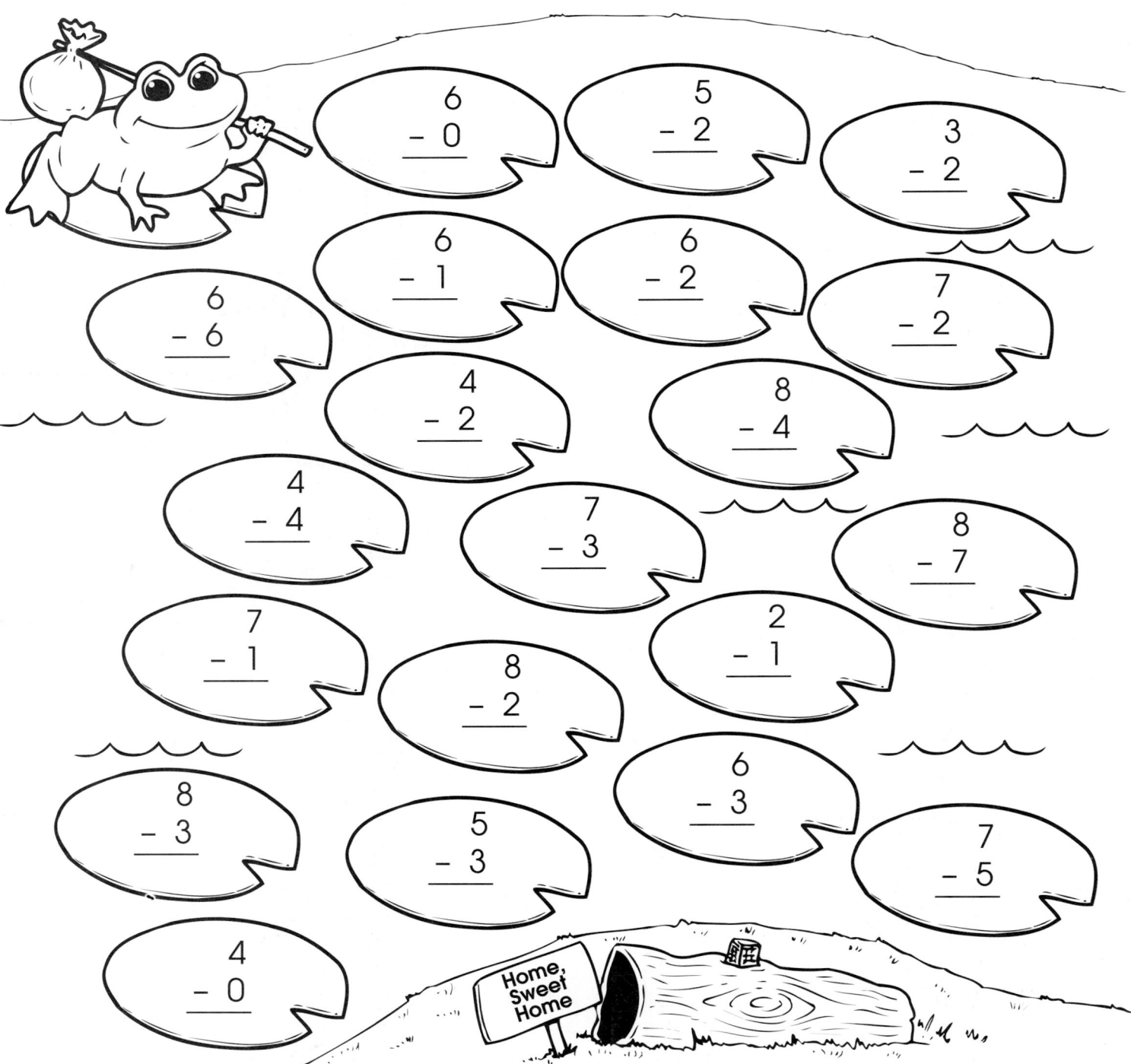

Up and Over

Name _____   Date _____

Subtract.
Color by the code.

8
− 4

6
− 2

5
− 1

5
− 3

8
− 1

6
− 4

1
− 1

6
− 0

5
− 5

4
− 3

3
− 2

8
− 3

7
− 2

7
− 5

7
− 1

6
− 5

7
− 7

8
− 7

8
− 6

7
− 0

8
− 5

8
− 2

7
− 4

2
− 1

5
− 0

The Spider Fact Family

Name _____ Date _____

Add and subtract.

4 + 3 = _____
7 − 4 = _____
3 + 4 = _____
7 − 3 = _____

6 + 2 = _____
8 − 2 = _____
2 + 6 = _____
8 − 6 = _____

2 + 5 = _____
7 − 2 = _____
5 + 2 = _____
7 − 5 = _____

2 + 4 = _____
6 − 4 = _____
4 + 2 = _____
6 − 2 = _____

5 + 3 = _____
8 − 3 = _____
3 + 5 = _____
8 − 5 = _____

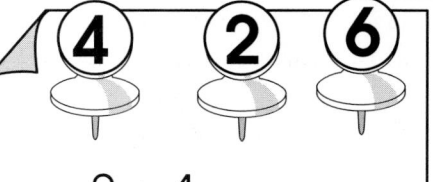

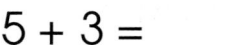

Birthday Surprises

Name _____ Date _____

Add and subtract.

2 + 1 = ____
3 − 2 = ____
1 + 2 = ____
3 − 1 = ____

5 + 1 = ____
6 − 1 = ____
1 + 5 = ____
6 − 5 = ____

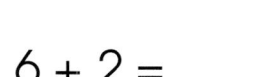

6 + 2 = ____
8 − 6 = ____
2 + 6 = ____
8 − 2 = ____

3 + 1 = ____
4 − 1 = ____
1 + 3 = ____
4 − 3 = ____

5 + 2 = ____
7 − 2 = ____
2 + 5 = ____
7 − 5 = ____

Fact families **27**

In Bloom

Name _____ Date _____

Subtract.
Color by the code.

8 − 6 = ____

5 − 0 = ____

8 − 5 = ____

9 − 3 = ____

7 − 1 = ____

9 − 4 = ____

6 − 4 = ____

9 − 5 = ____

9 − 6 = ____

9 − 7 = ____

6 − 1 = ____

6 − 3 = ____

7 − 2 = ____

7 − 3 = ____

6 − 0 = ____

8 − 2 = ____

7 − 5 = ____

8 − 4 = ____

9 − 2 = ____

7 − 0 = ____

8 − 1 = ____

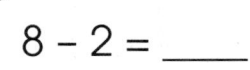

Color Code	
2—orange	5—yellow
3—blue	6—green
4—purple	7—brown

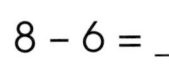

A Wild Ride

Name _____ Date _____

Subtract.
Color by the code.

Woo hoo!

9 – 5 = _____
6 – 2 = _____

1 – 0 = _____
7 – 6 = _____

8 – 3 = _____
5 – 0 = _____

8 – 5 = _____
4 – 1 = _____

5 – 3 = _____
9 – 7 = _____

9 – 2 = _____
8 – 1 = _____

8 – 4 = _____
4 – 0 = _____

9 – 3 = _____
7 – 1 = _____

9 – 6 = _____
6 – 3 = _____

7 – 2 = _____
9 – 4 = _____

9 – 1 = _____
8 – 0 = _____

3 – 1 = _____
8 – 6 = _____

Color Code
1 or 2—yellow
3 or 4—blue
5 or 6—green
7 or 8—red

Bunches of Bubbles

Name _____ Date _____

Subtract.
Cross off a matching answer.

$$\begin{array}{r} 7 \\ -\ 3 \\ \hline \end{array}$$

$$\begin{array}{r} 9 \\ -\ 4 \\ \hline \end{array}$$

$$\begin{array}{r} 8 \\ -\ 3 \\ \hline \end{array}$$

$$\begin{array}{r} 9 \\ -\ 3 \\ \hline \end{array}$$

$$\begin{array}{r} 6 \\ -\ 2 \\ \hline \end{array}$$

$$\begin{array}{r} 8 \\ -\ 4 \\ \hline \end{array}$$

$$\begin{array}{r} 9 \\ -\ 2 \\ \hline \end{array}$$

$$\begin{array}{r} 5 \\ -\ 3 \\ \hline \end{array}$$

$$\begin{array}{r} 7 \\ -\ 4 \\ \hline \end{array}$$

$$\begin{array}{r} 6 \\ -\ 5 \\ \hline \end{array}$$

$$\begin{array}{r} 8 \\ -\ 6 \\ \hline \end{array}$$

$$\begin{array}{r} 5 \\ -\ 2 \\ \hline \end{array}$$

$$\begin{array}{r} 9 \\ -\ 8 \\ \hline \end{array}$$

$$\begin{array}{r} 6 \\ -\ 4 \\ \hline \end{array}$$

$$\begin{array}{r} 5 \\ -\ 4 \\ \hline \end{array}$$

$$\begin{array}{r} 7 \\ -\ 5 \\ \hline \end{array}$$

$$\begin{array}{r} 6 \\ -\ 3 \\ \hline \end{array}$$

$$\begin{array}{r} 7 \\ -\ 6 \\ \hline \end{array}$$

$$\begin{array}{r} 4 \\ -\ 3 \\ \hline \end{array}$$

$$\begin{array}{r} 9 \\ -\ 6 \\ \hline \end{array}$$

$$\begin{array}{r} 8 \\ -\ 5 \\ \hline \end{array}$$

$$\begin{array}{r} 3 \\ -\ 1 \\ \hline \end{array}$$

$$\begin{array}{r} 9 \\ -\ 5 \\ \hline \end{array}$$

$$\begin{array}{r} 4 \\ -\ 2 \\ \hline \end{array}$$

$$\begin{array}{r} 8 \\ -\ 7 \\ \hline \end{array}$$

Answers

3	1	2	3	1	3	2	4	1
4	5	4	2	6	5	4	1	3
3	1	2	7	2	2	2	1	

Feathered Friend

Name _____   Date _____

Subtract.
Color by the code.

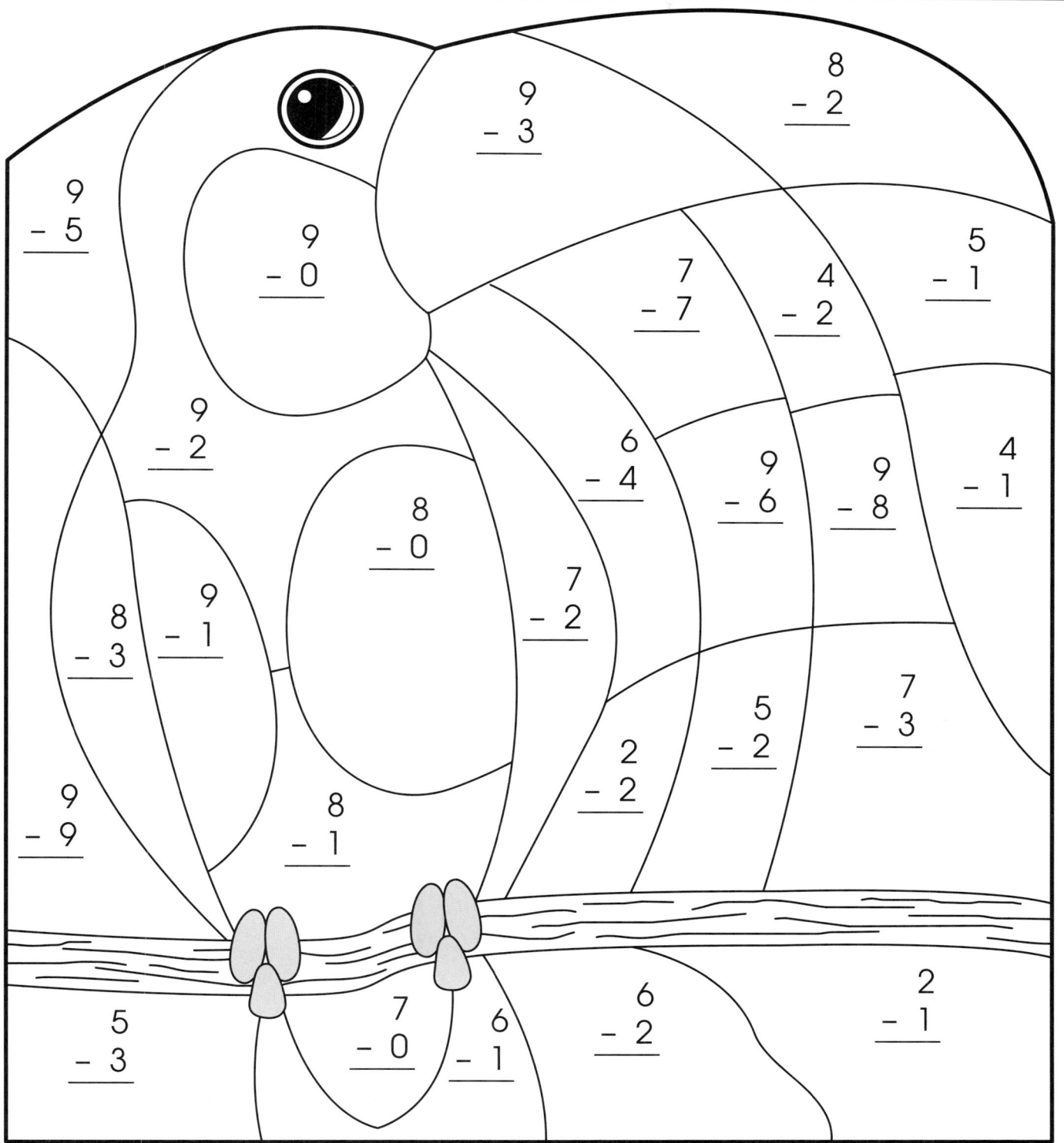

$$9 - 3$$

$$8 - 2$$

$$9 - 5$$

$$9 - 0$$

$$7 - 7$$

$$4 - 2$$

$$5 - 1$$

$$9 - 2$$

$$6 - 4$$

$$9 - 6$$

$$9 - 8$$

$$4 - 1$$

$$8 - 0$$

$$7 - 2$$

$$8 - 3$$

$$9 - 1$$

$$5 - 2$$

$$7 - 3$$

$$2 - 2$$

$$9 - 9$$

$$8 - 1$$

$$5 - 3$$

$$7 - 0$$

$$6 - 1$$

$$6 - 2$$

$$2 - 1$$

Super Shoppers

Name _____   Date _____

Read.
Write the math sentence.

Frozen Foods

He buys **8** 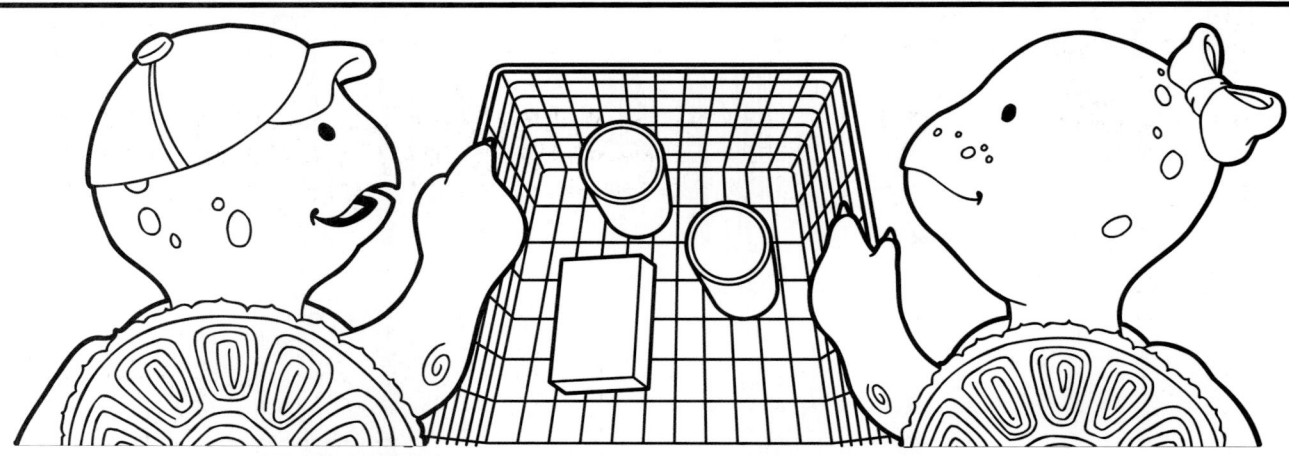.
He eats **5** .
How many are left?

_____ – _____ = _____

She gets **9** .
She mixes **3** .
How many are left?

_____ – _____ = _____

There are **9** for sale.
They buy **7** .
How many are left?

_____ – _____ = _____

She buys **8** .
She eats **2** .
How many are left?

_____ – _____ = _____

He buys **9** .
They eat **6** .
How many are left?

_____ – _____ = _____

There are **9** .
4 melt.
How many are left?

_____ – _____ = _____

Where's My Melon?

Name _____ Date _____

Subtract.

Help Crow find his watermelon.

If the answer is **4** or **5**, color the melon **green**.

10 – 5 = ___   10 – 1 = ___   9 – 2 = ___

10 – 7 = ___   9 – 4 = ___   8 – 2 = ___   10 – 3 = ___

9 – 0 = ___   9 – 5 = ___   10 – 6 = ___   8 – 5 = ___

10 – 2 = ___   9 – 8 = ___   8 – 4 = ___   10 – 8 = ___

7 – 1 = ___   10 – 4 = ___   9 – 5 = ___

Crow's Melon

Just the Right Spot

Name _____   Date _____

Subtract.
Color by the code.

8 – 0 = _____

9 – 0 = _____

8 – 1 = _____

8 – 3 = _____

10 – 0 = _____

9 – 2 = _____

7 – 0 = _____

7 – 2 = _____

9 – 1 = _____

10 – 1 = _____

6 – 0 = _____

10 – 2 = _____

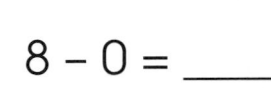
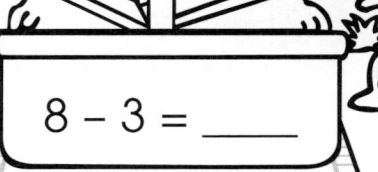
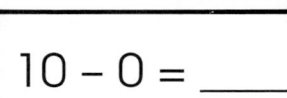
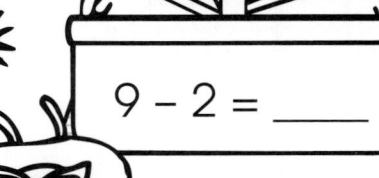

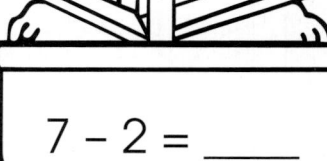
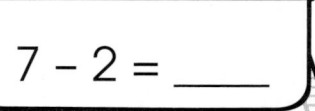
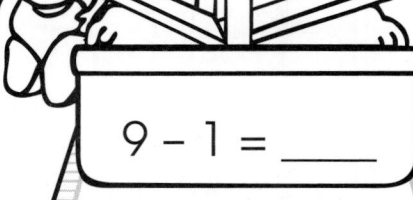

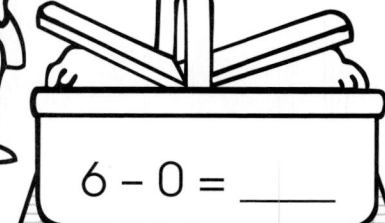
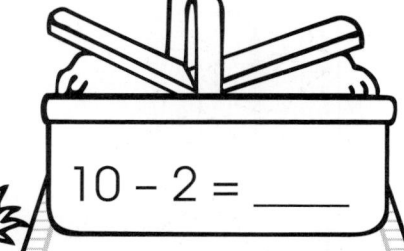

A Rich Fish

Name _____ Date _____

Subtract.
Match the letters to the numbered
lines below to solve the riddle.

8 − 3 I	10 − 1 G	9 − 4 I	7 − 3 S	8 − 2 F
10 − 4 F	10 − 7 L	9 − 2 D	10 − 2 H	7 − 2 I
9 − 1 H	9 − 5 S	10 − 0 O	9 − 3 F	10 − 5 I
9 − 6 L	8 − 1 D	10 − 6 S	8 − 5 L	10 − 3 D

**Which fish
is the richest?**

___ ___ ___ ___ ___ ___ ___ ___
 9   10   3   7   6   5   4   8

©The Education Center, Inc. • *Target Math Success* • TEC60826 • Key p. 130

Subtraction facts to 10 35

Smile!

Name _____ Date _____

Subtract.
Color by the code.

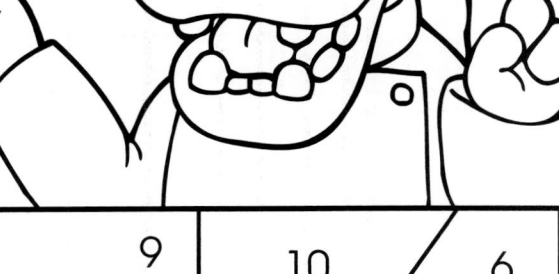

How many teeth does an adult human have?

Color Code
5 or 6—purple
7—yellow

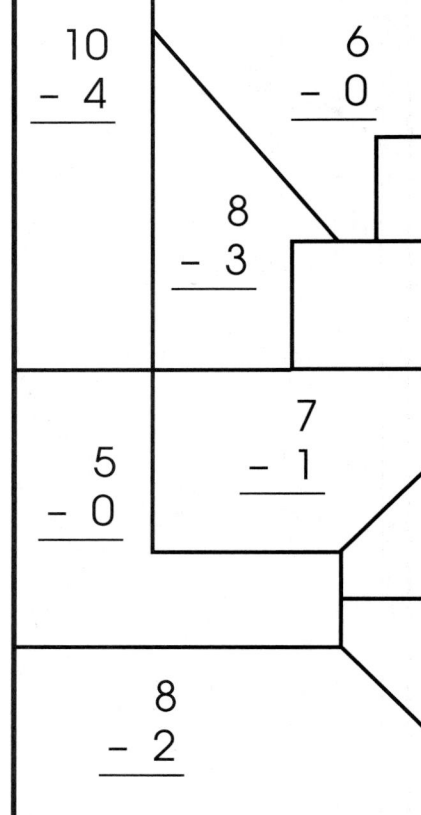

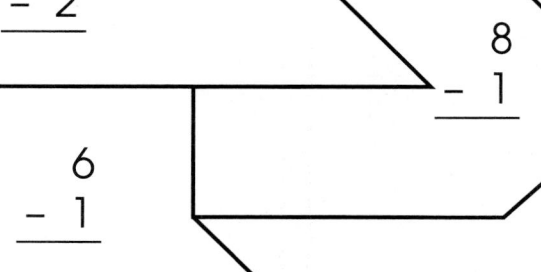

10 − 4	6 − 0

5 − 0

8 − 3

7 − 1

8 − 2

9 − 4

10 − 5

6 − 1

8 − 3

10 − 3

9 − 2

5 − 0

7 − 1

9 − 4

8 − 3

9 − 3

8 − 2

10 − 5

7 − 0

6 − 0

8 − 1

6 − 1

6 − 0

7 − 2

Favorite Flavors

Name _____   Date _____

Add and subtract.

Captain Sharkey's
SEASIDE ICE-CREAM SHACK

Menu
- Mackerel Fudge
- Bubble Chum
- Sardine Chip
- Octopustacio
- Squid Ripple

$10 - 1 =$ _____
$9 + 1 =$ _____
$10 - 9 =$ _____
$1 + 9 =$ _____

$8 - 2 =$ _____
$6 + 2 =$ _____
$8 - 6 =$ _____
$2 + 6 =$ _____

$7 - 4 =$ _____
$3 + 4 =$ _____
$7 - 3 =$ _____
$4 + 3 =$ _____

$9 - 6 =$ _____
$3 + 6 =$ _____
$9 - 3 =$ _____
$6 + 3 =$ _____

$9 - 7 =$ _____
$7 + 2 =$ _____
$9 - 2 =$ _____
$2 + 7 =$ _____

$10 - 2 =$ _____
$8 + 2 =$ _____
$10 - 8 =$ _____
$2 + 8 =$ _____

Wise With Numbers

Name _____   Date _____

Add and subtract.

8 − 3 = ____
5 + 3 = ____
8 − 5 = ____
3 + 5 = ____

9 − 8 = ____
1 + 8 = ____
9 − 1 = ____
8 + 1 = ____

9 − 5 = ____
4 + 5 = ____
9 − 4 = ____
5 + 4 = ____

10 − 3 = ____
7 + 3 = ____
10 − 7 = ____
3 + 7 = ____

8 − 1 = ____
7 + 1 = ____
8 − 7 = ____
1 + 7 = ____

10 − 4 = ____
4 + 6 = ____
10 − 6 = ____
6 + 4 = ____

7 − 2 = ____
5 + 2 = ____
7 − 5 = ____
2 + 5 = ____

10 − 2 = ____
8 + 2 = ____
10 − 8 = ____
2 + 8 = ____

Sunken Treasure

Name _____ Date _____

Subtract.
Cross off a matching answer.

$9 - 1 = $ _____ $11 - 3 = $ _____ $10 - 8 = $ _____

$8 - 3 = $ _____ $7 - 2 = $ _____ $11 - 5 = $ _____

$7 - 5 = $ _____ $6 - 4 = $ _____ $8 - 4 = $ _____

$10 - 9 = $ _____ $5 - 3 = $ _____ $9 - 5 = $ _____

$7 - 3 = $ _____ $11 - 8 = $ _____

$8 - 5 = $ _____ $10 - 3 = $ _____

$11 - 4 = $ _____ $9 - 6 = $ _____

$11 - 9 = $ _____ $8 - 1 = $ _____

$9 - 2 = $ _____ $11 - 6 = $ _____

$10 - 5 = $ _____ $9 - 7 = $ _____

8 2 6 1 4 7 5 2 7 8 2 5

3 5 4 7 4 3 2 3 2 2 5 7

Rrready to Go!

Name _____   Date _____

Subtract.
Color by the code.

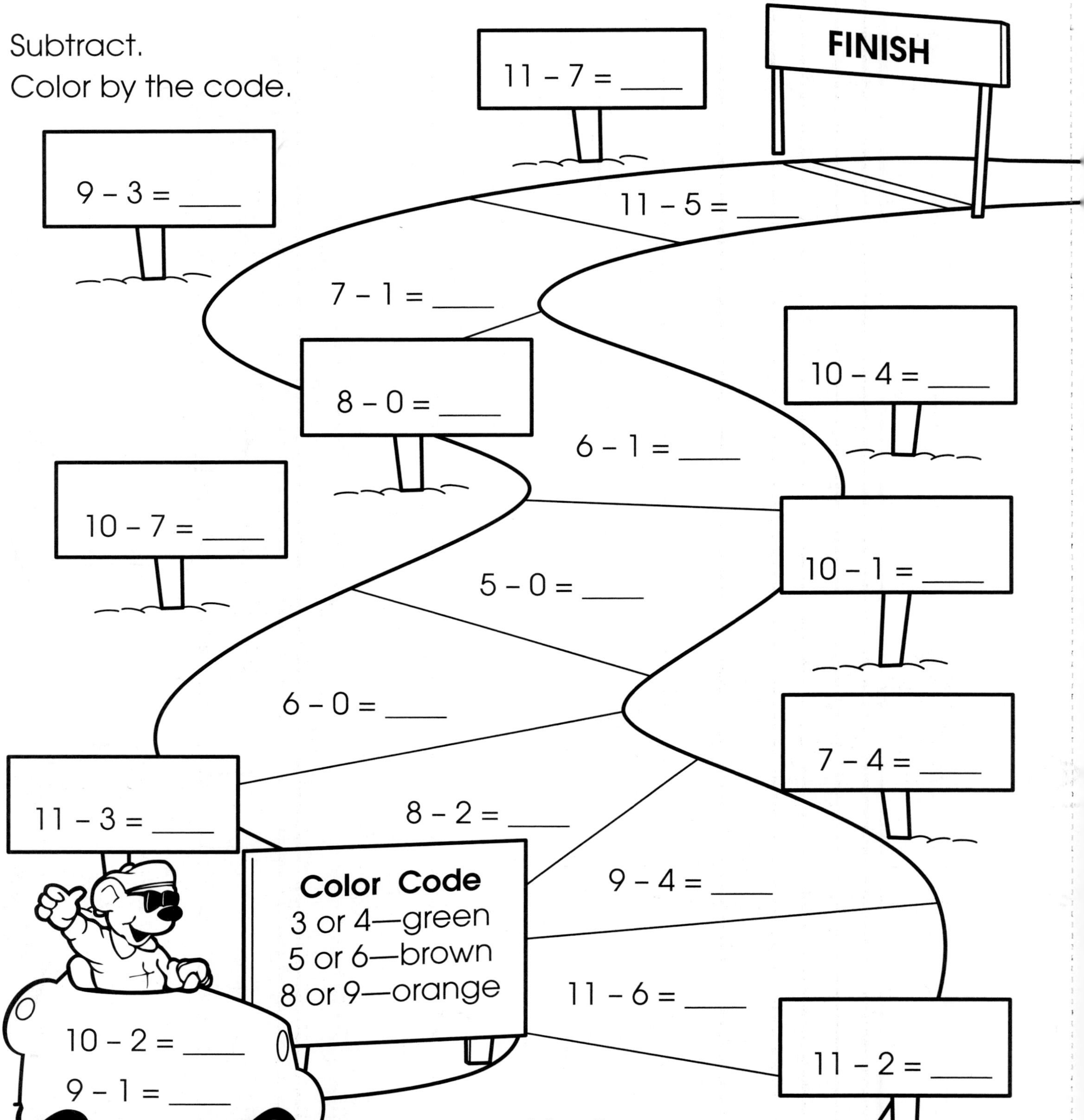

FINISH

$11 - 7 =$ _____

$9 - 3 =$ _____

$11 - 5 =$ _____

$7 - 1 =$ _____

$8 - 0 =$ _____

$10 - 4 =$ _____

$6 - 1 =$ _____

$10 - 7 =$ _____

$5 - 0 =$ _____

$10 - 1 =$ _____

$6 - 0 =$ _____

$7 - 4 =$ _____

$11 - 3 =$ _____

$8 - 2 =$ _____

Color Code
3 or 4—green
5 or 6—brown
8 or 9—orange

$9 - 4 =$ _____

$11 - 6 =$ _____

$10 - 2 =$ _____

$9 - 1 =$ _____

$11 - 2 =$ _____

$10 - 5 =$ _____

Apple-Picking Time

Name _____ Date _____

Subtract.
Color by the code.

$$10 - 0$$

$$10 - 2$$

$$9 - 6$$

$$10 - 1$$

$$9 - 0$$

$$11 - 2$$

$$10 - 7$$

$$9 - 1$$

$$8 - 5$$

$$11 - 3$$

$$10 - 3$$

$$9 - 2$$

$$9 - 5$$

$$10 - 5$$

$$6 - 0$$

$$10 - 4$$

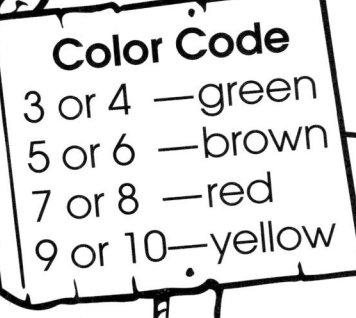

Color Code
3 or 4 —green
5 or 6 —brown
7 or 8 —red
9 or 10—yellow

$$11 - 7$$

$$10 - 6$$

$$11 - 8$$

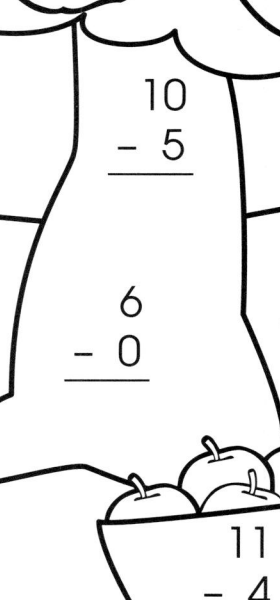

$$11 - 4$$

Off to the Clubhouse

Name _____ Date _____

Subtract.
Help Squirrel get to the clubhouse.
If the answer is **5, 6,** or **7,** color it **red.**

10 − 3	9 − 2	5 − 0	6 − 3
9 − 6	8 − 6	6 − 1	7 − 5
9 − 0	10 − 6	9 − 4	7 − 0	5 − 4
9 − 3	11 − 5	8 − 3	11 − 8	11 − 3
11 − 4	10 − 1	11 − 2	
7 − 2	5 − 0	11 − 6	

Clubhouse

It's a Cookout!

Name _____   Date _____

Read.
Write the math sentence.

There are 6 burgers.
1 does not have cheese.
How many burgers have cheese?

_____ – _____ = _____

11 burgers have pickles.
Ollie eats 3.
How many burgers are left?

_____ – _____ = _____

There are 10 friends.
7 go home.
How many friends are left?

_____ – _____ = _____

Ollie cooks 9 burgers.
His friends eat 7.
How many burgers are left?

_____ – _____ = _____

Ollie cooks 11 burgers.
He burns 6.
How many burgers are left?

_____ – _____ = _____

There are 8 burgers.
4 fall on the ground.
How many burgers are left?

_____ – _____ = _____

Yum! Sweet Treats

Name _____ Date _____

Read.
Write the math sentence.

Rabbit has 11 gumballs.
He sells 6.
How many gumballs are
    left?

_____ – _____ = _____

Rabbit has 9 lemon drops.
He gives away 2.
How many lemon drops
    are left?

_____ – _____ = _____

Rabbit has 11 chocolates.
He eats 8.
How many chocolates are
    left?

_____ – _____ = _____

Rabbit has 11 lollipops.
He sells 3.
How many lollipops are
    left?

_____ – _____ = _____

There are 10 gumballs.
Rabbit eats 2.
How many gumballs
    are left?

_____ – _____ = _____

Rabbit has 10 chocolates.
7 melt.
How many chocolates
    are left?

_____ – _____ = _____

Hoppin' and Poppin'

Name _____ Date _____

Look at the big number.
Circle **4** ways to make that number.

5
12 – 7
11 – 3
10 – 5
11 – 6
12 – 9
8 – 3

8
10 – 1
12 – 4
11 – 3
12 – 6
9 – 1
10 – 2

7
9 – 2
10 – 9
12 – 5
11 – 9
10 – 3
11 – 4

4
10 – 7
12 – 8
8 – 6
11 – 7
10 – 6
9 – 5

6
9 – 6
12 – 6
11 – 5
11 – 8
9 – 3
8 – 2

9
12 – 3
9 – 7
10 – 8
11 – 2
9 – 0
10 – 1

Animals Aloft

Name _____   Date _____

Subtract.
Color by the code.

12 − 9 = ____

10 − 3 = ____	9 − 4 = ____	9 − 5 = ____
12 − 8 = ____	11 − 4 = ____	12 − 7 = ____
10 − 2 = ____	11 − 6 = ____	11 − 7 = ____
12 − 6 = ____	10 − 6 = ____	10 − 5 = ____
9 − 1 = ____	9 − 3 = ____	9 − 6 = ____
10 − 7 = ____	12 − 4 = ____	11 − 5 = ____
11 − 3 = ____	10 − 4 = ____	11 − 8 = ____

Color Code
3 or 4 — red
5 or 6 — purple
7 or 8 — yellow

Crown Prince

Name _____ Date _____

Subtract.
Color a matching answer.

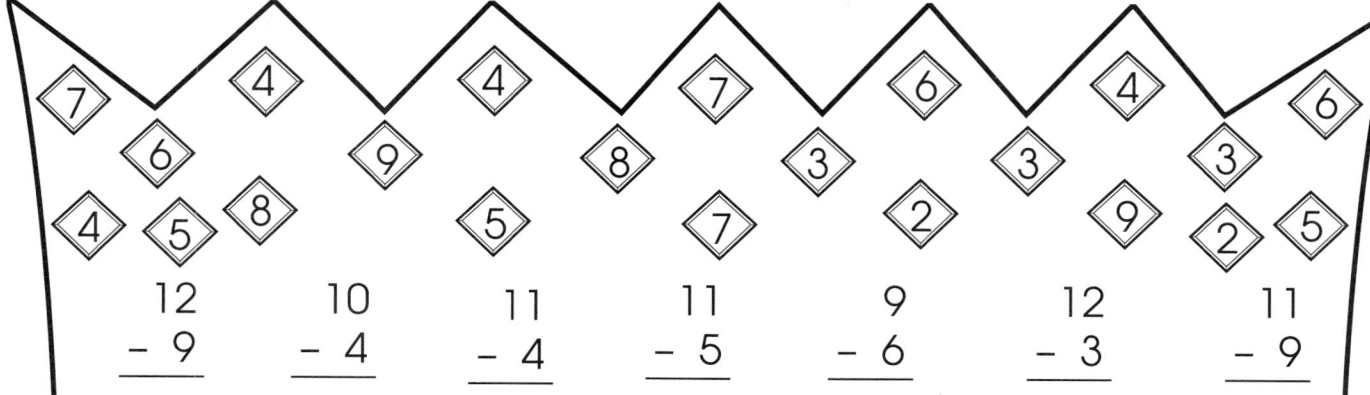

7	4	4	7	6	4	6
6	9	8	3	3	3	
4 5 8		5	7	2	9	2 5

12	10	11	11	9	12	11
− 9	− 4	− 4	− 5	− 6	− 3	− 9

12	10	11	9	12	10	11
− 6	− 8	− 7	− 2	− 5	− 6	− 3

12	11	10	9	11	10	12	12
− 8	− 2	− 7	− 5	− 6	− 5	− 7	− 4

Shells by the Sea

Name _____ Date _____

Subtract.
Color by the code.

$$10 - 6$$

$$11 - 5$$

$$9 - 1$$

$$10 - 5$$

$$11 - 8$$

$$10 - 7$$

$$12 - 5$$

$$9 - 6$$

$$10 - 3$$

$$12 - 7$$

$$11 - 4$$

$$9 - 5$$

$$12 - 8$$

$$11 - 7$$

$$10 - 4$$

Color Code
3 or 4—blue
5 or 6—green
7 or 8—orange

$$9 - 3$$

$$11 - 3$$

$$11 - 6$$

$$9 - 4$$

$$12 - 9$$

$$12 - 4$$

$$12 - 6$$

Subtraction facts to 12

Windy Facts

Name _____ Date _____

Add and subtract.

11 − 2 = ___
9 + 2 = ___
11 − 9 = ___
2 + 9 = ___

12 − 8 = ___
8 + 4 = ___
12 − 4 = ___
4 + 8 = ___

12 − 10 = ___
10 + 2 = ___
12 − 2 = ___
2 + 10 = ___

11 − 4 = ___
7 + 4 = ___
11 − 7 = ___
4 + 7 = ___

12 − 6 = ___
6 + 6 = ___

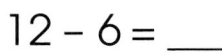

10 − 5 = ___
5 + 5 = ___

Smooth Sailing

Name _____ Date _____

Add and subtract.

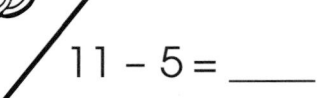

11 – 5 = ____   11 – 6 = ____

6 + 5 = ____   5 + 6 = ____

5, 6, 11

10 – 4 = ____   10 – 6 = ____

4 + 6 = ____   6 + 4 = ____

4, 6, 10

11 – 3 = ____   11 – 8 = ____

3 + 8 = ____   8 + 3 = ____

3, 8, 11

12 – 5 = ____   12 – 7 = ____

5 + 7 = ____   7 + 5 = ____

5, 7, 12

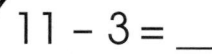

Top Dog!

Name _____ Date _____

Subtract.
Color by the code.

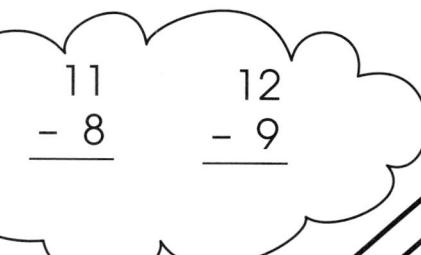

11   12
- 8   - 9

Color Code

3—white   6—green
4—red   7—orange
5—blue   8—yellow
        9—purple

13
- 9

14   11   13
- 9   - 5   - 6

11   14   10   13   14   9
- 3   - 5   - 6   - 4   - 6   - 5

12   14   12   13
- 3   - 8   - 6   - 8

14   10   11   12
- 7   - 5   - 2   - 4

A Little Monkey Business

Name _____ Date _____

Subtract.
Help Mr. Monkey get to his bananas.
If the answer is **5, 6,** or **7,** color it **green.**

12 − 7	11 − 6	14 − 8	13 − 9	14 − 5
11 − 7	11 − 3	13 − 5	14 − 7	11 − 8	12 − 3
14 − 6	12 − 9	13 − 8	13 − 4	11 − 9	10 − 8
12 − 8	12 − 5	12 − 6	13 − 7		

A Froggy Feast

Name _____ Date _____

Subtract.
If the answer is **6** or **7**, color it **green**.
Read the riddle answer.

What do frogs eat for breakfast?

Fishy Facts

Name _____   Date _____

Look at the big number.
Circle **4** ways to make
    that number.

7

14 – 7
12 – 6
11 – 4
10 – 3
13 – 6
11 – 3

9

13 – 4
11 – 2
11 – 7
10 – 1
13 – 7
14 – 5

8

14 – 6
12 – 6
13 – 5
11 – 8
12 – 4
11 – 3

6

11 – 5
10 – 6
14 – 8
11 – 6
13 – 7
12 – 6

A "Bear-y" Bright Light

Name _____ Date _____

Read.
Write the math sentence.

There are 12 steps.
Bear climbs 8.
How many steps are left?

____ − ____ = ____

There are 13 boats at sea.
6 come to the shore.
How many boats are left?

____ − ____ = ____

There are 13 whales.
7 swim away.
How many whales are left?

____ − ____ = ____

There are 14 lights.
5 burn out.
How many lights are left?

____ − ____ = ____

There are 14 birds.
7 fly away.
How many birds are left?

____ − ____ = ____

There are 12 workers.
6 go home.
How many workers are left?

____ − ____ = ____

Birthday Bash!

Name _____   Date _____

Read.
Write the math sentence.

There are 13 games.
5 are played.
How many games are left?

_____ - _____ = _____

There are 12 balloons.
7 pop.
How many balloons are left?

_____ - _____ = _____

There are 12 candles.
3 break.
How many candles are left?

_____ - _____ = _____

There are 14 gifts.
8 are opened.
How many gifts are left?

_____ - _____ = _____

There are 13 pieces of cake.
9 are eaten.
How many pieces are left?

_____ - _____ = _____

There are 14 guests.
5 go home.
How many guests are left?

_____ - _____ = _____

Happy Birthday!

Story problems: subtraction facts to 14

Ahoy, Matey!

Name _____ Date _____

Subtract.
Color by the code.

Color Code
3 or 4 — blue
5 — yellow
6 or 7 — red
8 or 9 — brown

$$\begin{array}{r} 14 \\ -\ 9 \\ \hline \end{array} \qquad \begin{array}{r} 13 \\ -\ 8 \\ \hline \end{array}$$

$$\begin{array}{r} 16 \\ -\ 9 \\ \hline \end{array} \qquad \begin{array}{r} 15 \\ -\ 8 \\ \hline \end{array}$$

$$\begin{array}{r} 14 \\ -\ 8 \\ \hline \end{array} \qquad \begin{array}{r} 15 \\ -\ 9 \\ \hline \end{array}$$

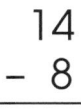

SS Gator

$$\begin{array}{r} 16 \\ -\ 7 \\ \hline \end{array} \qquad \begin{array}{r} 13 \\ -\ 5 \\ \hline \end{array} \qquad \begin{array}{r} 14 \\ -\ 5 \\ \hline \end{array}$$

$$\begin{array}{r} 15 \\ -\ 7 \\ \hline \end{array} \qquad \begin{array}{r} 13 \\ -\ 4 \\ \hline \end{array}$$

$$\begin{array}{r} 15 \\ -\ 6 \\ \hline \end{array} \qquad \begin{array}{r} 14 \\ -\ 6 \\ \hline \end{array} \qquad \begin{array}{r} 16 \\ -\ 8 \\ \hline \end{array}$$

$$\begin{array}{r} 13 \\ -\ 9 \\ \hline \end{array} \qquad \begin{array}{r} 12 \\ -\ 9 \\ \hline \end{array} \qquad \begin{array}{r} 11 \\ -\ 7 \\ \hline \end{array} \qquad \begin{array}{r} 12 \\ -\ 8 \\ \hline \end{array}$$

Space Sightings

Name _____   Date _____

Subtract.
Cross off a matching answer.

$$16 - 9$$ $$11 - 4$$ $$14 - 7$$

$$12 - 9$$ $$16 - 8$$ $$15 - 9$$

$$14 - 8$$ $$12 - 5$$ $$16 - 7$$ $$15 - 8$$ $$14 - 9$$

$$11 - 3$$ $$13 - 8$$ $$15 - 7$$ $$13 - 7$$ $$15 - 6$$

$$12 - 7$$ $$14 - 5$$

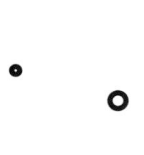

Answers

8 9 6 7 5 3 8 9

7 5 7 8 6 7 5 9 7 6

Subtraction facts to 16

No More Honey!

Name _____   Date _____

Subtract.
Match the letters to the numbered
lines below to solve the riddle.

16 − 9 E	15 − 7 S	10 − 9 H	13 − 6 E	13 − 7 T
14 − 8 T	13 − 8 W	15 − 8 E	12 − 8 U	15 − 6 A
16 − 7 A	16 − 8 S	11 − 9 D	11 − 8 F	14 − 7 E
14 − 9 W	12 − 5 E	13 − 5 S	14 − 5 A	13 − 4 A
11 − 7 U	14 − 6 S	12 − 9 F	13 − 9 U	15 − 9 T

Why couldn't the teddy bear finish his honey?

___ ___   ___ ___ ___ ___
 1   7   5   9   8

___ ___ ___ ___ ___ ___ ___ !
 8   6   4   3   3   7   2

Ready to Camp!

Subtract.
Help Randy Racoon find his tent.
If the answer is **6** or **7,** color the tent **yellow.**

14 − 8

16 − 9

15 − 6

12 − 7

16 − 7

15 − 8

14 − 9

13 − 6

13 − 7

15 − 9

13 − 5

14 − 7

13 − 9

14 − 5

15 − 7

Randy's
Tent

Super Scoopers

Name _____ Date _____

Add and subtract.

16 – 9 = ____

7 + 9 = ____

16 – 7 = ____

9 + 7 = ____

14 – 9 = ____

5 + 9 = ____

14 – 5 = ____

9 + 5 = ____

15 – 8 = ____

7 + 8 = ____

15 – 7 = ____

8 + 7 = ____

13 – 7 = ____

6 + 7 = ____

13 – 6 = ____

7 + 6 = ____

14 – 8 = ____

6 + 8 = ____

14 – 6 = ____

8 + 6 = ____

15 – 9 = ____

6 + 9 = ____

15 – 6 = ____

9 + 6 = ____

Barnyard Buddies

Name _____ Date _____

Add and subtract.

15 − 8 = _____

7 + 8 = _____

15 − 7 = _____

8 + 7 = _____

16 − 9 = _____

7 + 9 = _____

16 − 7 = _____

9 + 7 = _____

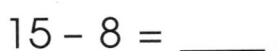

15 − 9 = _____

9 + 6 = _____

14 − 8 = _____

6 + 8 = _____

14 − 6 = _____

8 + 6 = _____

12 − 9 = _____

3 + 9 = _____

12 − 3 = _____

9 + 3 = _____

15 − 6 = _____

6 + 9 = _____

14 − 9 = _____

9 + 5 = _____

14 − 5 = _____

5 + 9 = _____

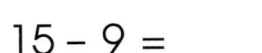

Round 'em Up, Cowboy!

Name _____ Date _____

Subtract.
Cross off a matching answer.

16 − 7	14 − 9	14 − 8	17 − 8	13 − 7	16 − 9
14 − 6	16 − 8	18 − 9	15 − 8	14 − 7	15 − 6
15 − 9	14 − 5	13 − 8	13 − 4	15 − 7	17 − 9

Answers

9 9 6 7 8 9
8 5 9 9 7 8
6 8 5 9 6 7

Hot off the Griddle!

Name _____   Date _____

Subtract.
Color by the code.

18 − 9 16 − 8	13 − 7 14 − 8	15 − 8 10 − 4	13 − 5 14 − 6
12 − 6 14 − 7	16 − 7 15 − 6	14 − 5 13 − 4	11 − 4 15 − 9
12 − 3 11 − 2	16 − 9 13 − 6	11 − 5 10 − 3	12 − 4 11 − 3

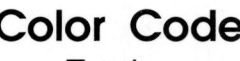

Color Code
6 or 7—brown
8 or 9—yellow

©The Education Center, Inc. • *Target Math Success* • TEC60826 • Key p. 133

Say, "Ah..."

Name _____ Date _____

Subtract.
Color by the code.

Color Code
2 or 3 — blue
4 or 5 — green ◯
6 or 7 — orange
8 or 9 — yellow

13
− 9

12
− 7

8
− 4

9
− 5

12
− 8

10
− 6

11
− 7

9
− 4

12
− 9

11
− 9

10
− 5

17
− 9

17
− 8

10
− 3

12
− 6

8
− 6

10
− 8

Moose on the Loose

Name _____

Subtract.
Color by the code.

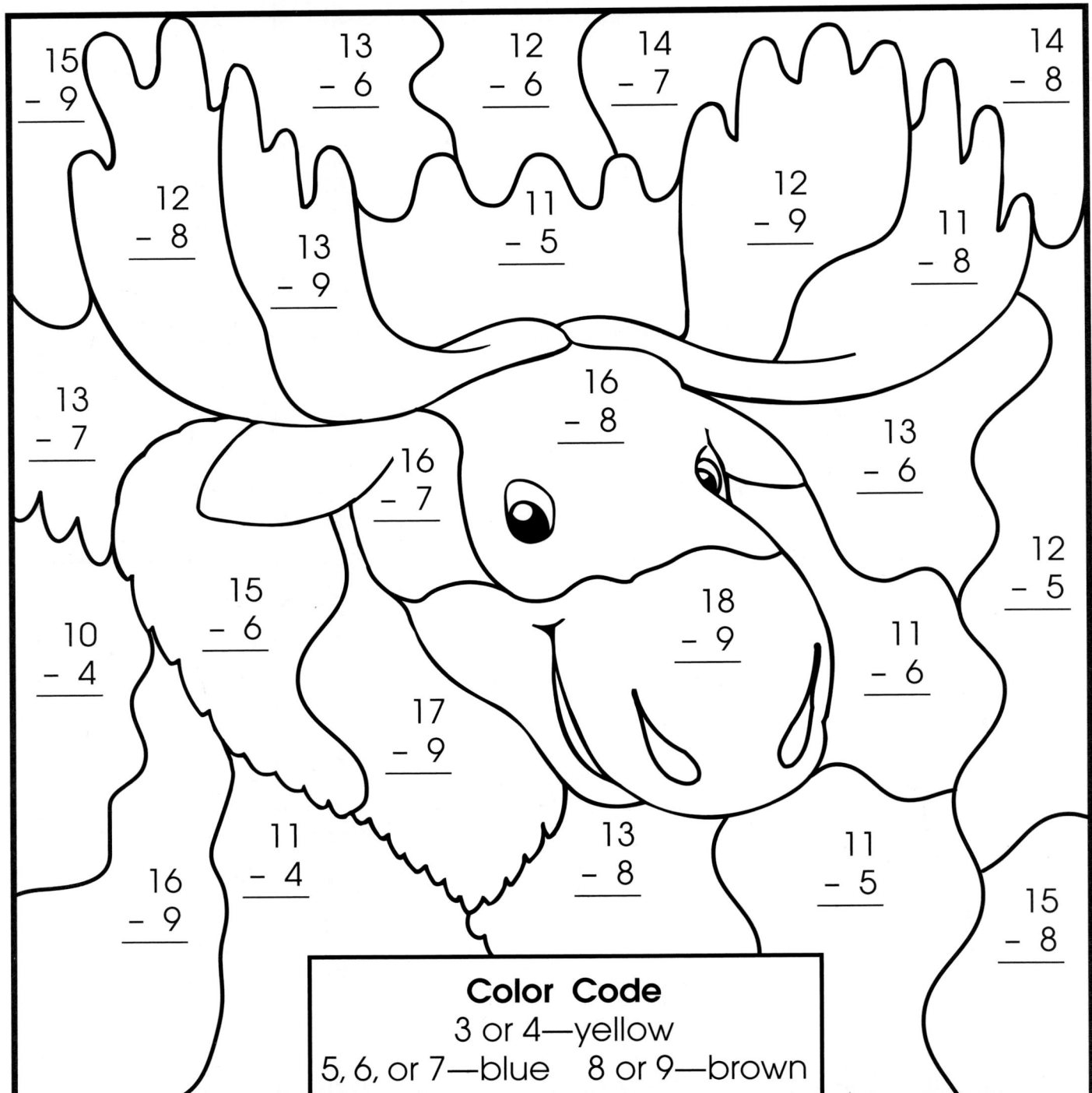

15
− 9

13
− 6

12
− 6

14
− 7

14
− 8

12
− 8

13
− 9

11
− 5

12
− 9

11
− 8

13
− 7

16
− 7

16
− 8

13
− 6

15
− 6

18
− 9

11
− 6

12
− 5

10
− 4

17
− 9

16
− 9

11
− 4

13
− 8

11
− 5

15
− 8

Color Code
3 or 4—yellow
5, 6, or 7—blue   8 or 9—brown

Hey, Mom! Watch Me!

Name _____ Date _____

Read.
Write the math sentence.

17 frogs eat by the pond. 9 leave to take a nap. How many frogs are left? _____ − _____ = _____	16 ducks swim in the pond. 7 get out. How many ducks are left? _____ − _____ = _____
14 ducks are asleep. 8 go to play. How many ducks are left? _____ − _____ = _____	There are 18 plants. 9 wilt. How many plants are left? _____ − _____ = _____
There are 15 flies. A frog eats 7. How many flies are left? _____ − _____ = _____	There are 16 lily pads. 9 float away. How many lily pads are left? _____ − _____ = _____

Great Teamwork!

Name _____ Date _____

Read.
Write the math sentence.

Crab has 18 shells. He buries 9. How many shells are left? ____ – ____ = ____	There are 17 starfish. 8 go home. How many starfish are left? ____ – ____ = ____
Octopus has 15 flags. He uses 9. How many flags are left? ____ – ____ = ____	There are 14 pebbles on the sand castle. 6 fall off. How many pebbles are left? ____ – ____ = ____
Starfish has 16 sticks. He loses 9. How many sticks are left? ____ – ____ = ____	Crab finds 15 pieces of seaweed. 8 float away. How many pieces are left? ____ – ____ = ____

Mixed Subtraction and Addition Practice

Mixed Subtraction and Addition Practice

Table of Contents

See pages 104–125 for corresponding parent communications and student checkups (minitests) for the skills listed above.

A "Mouse-ful" of Cookies

Name _____ Date _____

Add and subtract.
Color by the code.

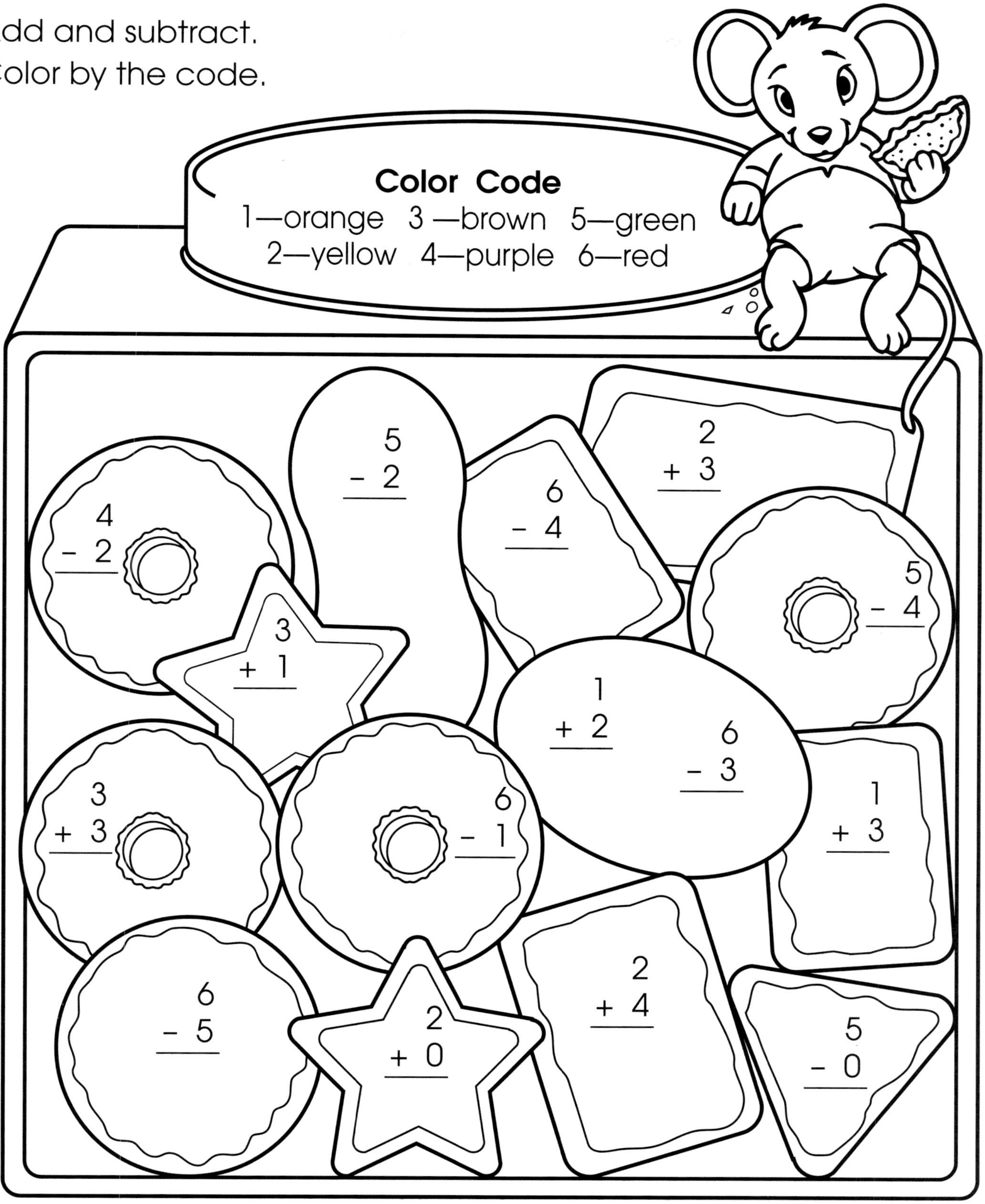

Color Code
1—orange 3—brown 5—green
2—yellow 4—purple 6—red

$$5 - 2$$

$$4 - 2$$

$$6 - 4$$

$$2 + 3$$

$$3 + 1$$

$$5 - 4$$

$$1 + 2$$

$$6 - 3$$

$$3 + 3$$

$$6 - 1$$

$$1 + 3$$

$$6 - 5$$

$$2 + 0$$

$$2 + 4$$

$$5 - 0$$

Munching on Mixed Facts

Name _____   Date _____

Add and subtract.
Circle each answer in the picture.

5 + 1 = ____   5 − 4 = ____   2 + 1 = ____   1 + 4 = ____

4 − 2 = ____   3 + 1 = ____   4 − 4 = ____   3 + 3 = ____

6 − 3 = ____   5 − 2 = ____   4 + 2 = ____   6 − 4 = ____

3 + 2 = ____   2 + 4 = ____   6 − 5 = ____   3 − 1 = ____

0 + 3 = ____   6 − 2 = ____   3 − 3 = ____   2 + 2 = ____

Mixed practice to 6

©The Education Center, Inc. • *Target Math Success* • TEC60826 • Key p. 134

Jungle Friends

Name _____   Date _____

Read.
Write the math sentence.

2 monkeys are in the jungle.
4 more come.
How many monkeys in all?   _____ + _____ = _____

A monkey eats 3 bananas.
It eats 2 more.
How many bananas in all?   _____ + _____ = _____

The giraffe sees 6 leaves.
It eats 4 leaves.
How many leaves are left?   _____ – _____ = _____

There are 3 lions in the jungle.
3 more come.
How many lions in all?   _____ + _____ = _____

5 elephants are swimming.
3 go home.
How many elephants are left? _____ – _____ = _____

There are 4 plants.
The elephant eats 2.
How many plants are left?   _____ – _____ = _____

Feeling the Rhythm

Name _____ Date _____

Add and subtract.
Color by the code.

5
+ 2
___

8
- 7
___

7
- 6
___

4
+ 3
___

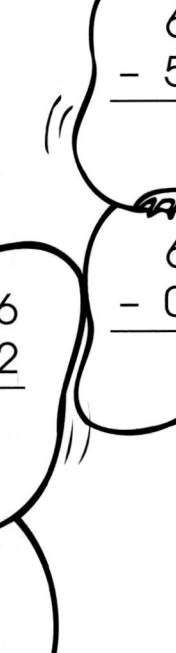

7
- 4
___

6
+ 2
___

1
+ 6
___

7
- 1
___

6
- 5
___

7
- 2
___

6
- 0
___

5
- 3
___

8
- 5
___

5
- 4
___

8
- 0
___

5
- 1
___

7
- 0
___

8
- 2
___

8
- 3
___

5
+ 3
___

8
- 1
___

7
- 5
___

6
- 4
___

7
+ 1
___

Color Code

1 or 2—orange   3 or 4—purple

5 or 6—yellow   7 or 8—green

To Market, to Market

Name _____ Date _____

Add and subtract.
Help Piggy get to the market.
If the answer is **4, 5,** or **6,** color the space **yellow.**

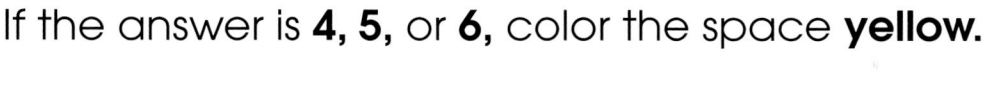

			1 + 7

8 − 3	3 + 2	7 − 6	8 − 5

7 − 7	6 + 1	1 + 4	3 + 5	6 − 5

7 − 4	1 + 5	8 − 2	8 − 7	4 + 4

6 − 3	2 + 4	0 + 8	6 + 2	8 − 8

7 + 0	6 − 2	2 + 5

6 − 4	7 − 3	3 + 3

PORKY'S MARKET

Play Ball!

Name _____ Date _____

Read.
Write the math sentence.

The team has 8 bats. 2 break. How many bats are left? 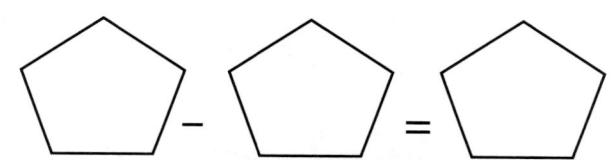	The pitcher chews 4 pieces of gum. Then he chews 3 more. How many pieces of gum in all? 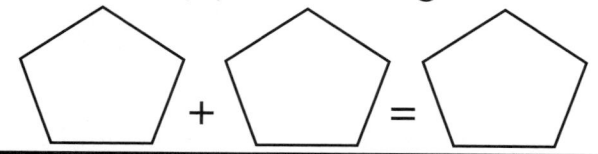
The catcher catches 7 balls. He drops 2. How many balls are left? 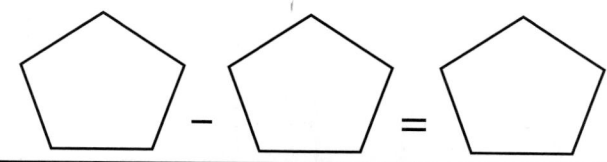	Coach calls out 7 rules. Then he calls out 1 more. How many rules in all? 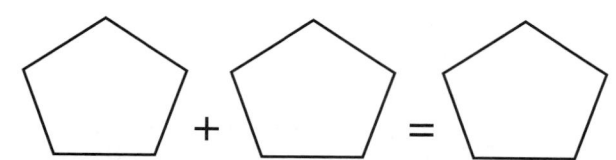
The player hits 5 balls. Then he hits 3 more. How many balls in all? 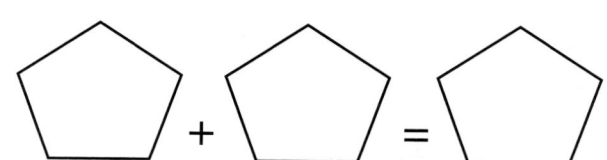	The team buys 8 caps. 3 get lost. How many caps are left? 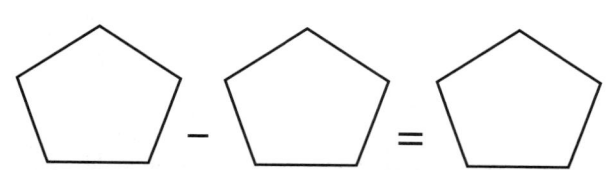

Story problems: mixed practice to 8

Dragon's Math Castle

Name _____   Date _____

Add or subtract.
Color by the code.

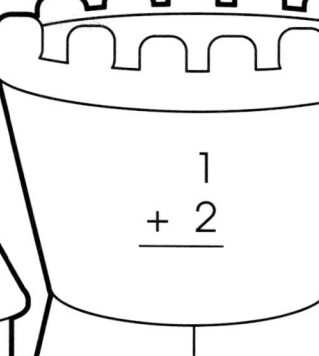

$$1 + 2$$

$$9 - 4$$

$$3 + 6$$

$$7 - 0$$

$$9 - 1$$

$$10 - 0$$

$$5 - 3$$

$$7 - 4$$

$$8 - 3$$

$$2 + 4$$

$$10 - 9$$

$$9 - 2$$

$$2 + 2$$

Color Code
1 or 2—blue   3 or 4—green
5 or 6—yellow   7 or 8—red
9 or 10—orange

$$2 + 6$$

$$8 - 5$$

$$4 + 3$$

$$9 - 7$$

$$8 - 2$$

$$9 - 5$$

Mixed practice to 10 77

Dinner Delivery

Name _____ Date _____

Add or subtract.
Help the ant get home.
If the answer is **4** or **5**,
  color the brick
  red.

7 − 2	10 − 8

9 − 8	4 + 6	7 + 2	4 + 1

8 − 5	3 + 1	9 − 4	4 + 4

5 + 2	10 − 5	3 + 6	9 − 2

8 − 4	7 − 4	8 − 2	1 + 6

3 + 3	2 + 3	9 − 5	0 + 8

0 + 5	4 + 2	7 + 3

Mixed practice to 10

Al E. Gator

Name _____ Date _____

Read.
Write the math sentence.

Al has 10 stuffed animals in bed.
He puts 7 on the floor.
How many animals are left?

_____ – _____ = _____

Al reads 4 stories.
Then he reads 6 more.
How many stories in all?

_____ + _____ = _____

Al has 6 blankets on the bed.
He takes off 2.
How many blankets are left?

_____ – _____ = _____

Al hears 3 noises.
Then he hears 6 more.
How many noises in all?

_____ + _____ = _____

Al gets 9 glasses of water.
He drinks 4.
How many glasses are left?

_____ – _____ = _____

Al has 8 brothers.
He has 2 sisters.
How many in all?

_____ + _____ = _____

Al has 10 pillows in bed.
2 fall on the floor.
How many pillows are left?

_____ – _____ = _____

Al sleeps for 7 hours.
Then he sleeps for 1 more.
How many hours in all?

_____ + _____ = _____

Story problems: mixed practice to 10

High-Flying Facts

Name _____ Date _____

Add and subtract.
Color by the code.

Color Code
4, 5, or 6—blue
7, 8, or 9—green
10, 11, or 12—yellow

12	11	10
− 8	− 5	− 5

9	10	7
+ 2	− 0	+ 5

12	5	11
− 4	+ 4	− 4

10	12	11
− 4	− 7	− 7

3	5	7
+ 9	+ 6	+ 3

11	12	11
− 2	− 5	− 3

Jungle Paradise

Name _____   Date _____

Add and subtract.
Cross off a matching answer.

$$\begin{array}{r} 12 \\ -\ 4 \\ \hline \end{array} \qquad \begin{array}{r} 6 \\ +\ 5 \\ \hline \end{array}$$

$$\begin{array}{r} 5 \\ +\ 7 \\ \hline \end{array}$$

$$\begin{array}{r} 3 \\ +\ 9 \\ \hline \end{array}$$

$$\begin{array}{r} 11 \\ -\ 2 \\ \hline \end{array} \qquad \begin{array}{r} 12 \\ -\ 6 \\ \hline \end{array}$$

11   12   8   12   6   9

$$\begin{array}{r} 11 \\ -\ 9 \\ \hline \end{array} \quad \begin{array}{r} 12 \\ -\ 5 \\ \hline \end{array} \quad \begin{array}{r} 12 \\ -\ 9 \\ \hline \end{array}$$

$$\begin{array}{r} 5 \\ +\ 6 \\ \hline \end{array} \quad \begin{array}{r} 4 \\ +\ 8 \\ \hline \end{array} \quad \begin{array}{r} 10 \\ -\ 9 \\ \hline \end{array}$$

$$\begin{array}{r} 12 \\ -\ 3 \\ \hline \end{array} \quad \begin{array}{r} 11 \\ -\ 7 \\ \hline \end{array} \quad \begin{array}{r} 11 \\ -\ 4 \\ \hline \end{array}$$

3   2   11   1   7   4   12   7   9

$$\begin{array}{r} 12 \\ -\ 7 \\ \hline \end{array} \quad \begin{array}{r} 9 \\ +\ 3 \\ \hline \end{array}$$

$$\begin{array}{r} 11 \\ -\ 6 \\ \hline \end{array} \quad \begin{array}{r} 7 \\ +\ 5 \\ \hline \end{array} \quad \begin{array}{r} 12 \\ -\ 8 \\ \hline \end{array}$$

$$\begin{array}{r} 4 \\ +\ 6 \\ \hline \end{array} \quad \begin{array}{r} 11 \\ -\ 3 \\ \hline \end{array}$$

12   5   5   4   12   8   10

Pete the Pretzel Pal

Name _____   Date _____

Read.
Write the math sentence.

Pete put 6 pretzels on the tray.
He adds 6 more.
How many pretzels in all?

_____ + _____ = _____

12 pretzels are on the tray.
4 fall off.
How many pretzels are
    left?

_____ - _____ = _____

Pete has 12 salty pretzels.
He eats 9.
How many pretzels are left?

_____ - _____ = _____

8 sugar pretzels are in the
    oven.
Pete adds 3 more.
How many pretzels in all?

_____ + _____ = _____

Pete rolls 11 pretzels in cinnamon.
He gives 4 away.
How many pretzels are left?

_____ - _____ = _____

7 pretzels are on the table.
Pete adds 5 more.
How many pretzels in all?

_____ + _____ = _____

"SSSuper" Math

Name _____ Date _____

Add and subtract.
Color by the code.

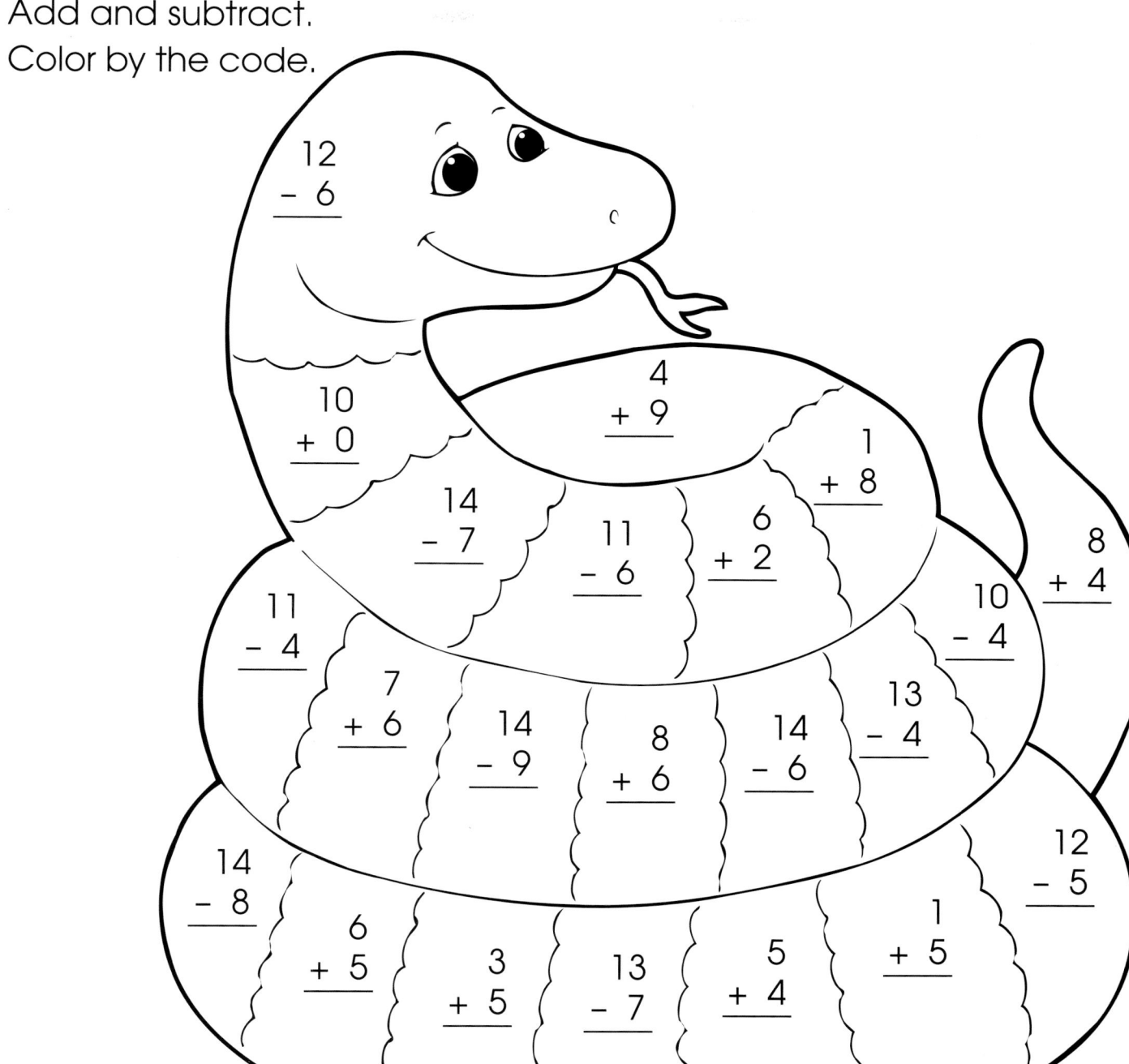

$\begin{array}{r} 12 \\ -\ 6 \\ \hline \end{array}$

$\begin{array}{r} 10 \\ +\ 0 \\ \hline \end{array}$

$\begin{array}{r} 4 \\ +\ 9 \\ \hline \end{array}$

$\begin{array}{r} 1 \\ +\ 8 \\ \hline \end{array}$

$\begin{array}{r} 14 \\ -\ 7 \\ \hline \end{array}$

$\begin{array}{r} 11 \\ -\ 6 \\ \hline \end{array}$

$\begin{array}{r} 6 \\ +\ 2 \\ \hline \end{array}$

$\begin{array}{r} 8 \\ +\ 4 \\ \hline \end{array}$

$\begin{array}{r} 11 \\ -\ 4 \\ \hline \end{array}$

$\begin{array}{r} 10 \\ -\ 4 \\ \hline \end{array}$

$\begin{array}{r} 7 \\ +\ 6 \\ \hline \end{array}$

$\begin{array}{r} 14 \\ -\ 9 \\ \hline \end{array}$

$\begin{array}{r} 8 \\ +\ 6 \\ \hline \end{array}$

$\begin{array}{r} 14 \\ -\ 6 \\ \hline \end{array}$

$\begin{array}{r} 13 \\ -\ 4 \\ \hline \end{array}$

$\begin{array}{r} 14 \\ -\ 8 \\ \hline \end{array}$

$\begin{array}{r} 12 \\ -\ 5 \\ \hline \end{array}$

$\begin{array}{r} 6 \\ +\ 5 \\ \hline \end{array}$

$\begin{array}{r} 3 \\ +\ 5 \\ \hline \end{array}$

$\begin{array}{r} 13 \\ -\ 7 \\ \hline \end{array}$

$\begin{array}{r} 5 \\ +\ 4 \\ \hline \end{array}$

$\begin{array}{r} 1 \\ +\ 5 \\ \hline \end{array}$

Color Code

5 or 6—green   9, 10, or 11—purple
7 or 8—yellow   12, 13, or 14—orange

Mixed practice to 14 83

Chicken Chase

Name _____ Date _____

Add and subtract.
Color a matching answer in the picture.

$$\begin{array}{r} 5 \\ + 9 \\ \hline \end{array}$$ $$\begin{array}{r} 12 \\ - 9 \\ \hline \end{array}$$ $$\begin{array}{r} 5 \\ + 6 \\ \hline \end{array}$$ $$\begin{array}{r} 7 \\ + 7 \\ \hline \end{array}$$ $$\begin{array}{r} 13 \\ - 8 \\ \hline \end{array}$$

$$\begin{array}{r} 5 \\ + 8 \\ \hline \end{array}$$ $$\begin{array}{r} 14 \\ - 8 \\ \hline \end{array}$$ $$\begin{array}{r} 4 \\ + 7 \\ \hline \end{array}$$ $$\begin{array}{r} 14 \\ - 5 \\ \hline \end{array}$$ $$\begin{array}{r} 3 \\ + 9 \\ \hline \end{array}$$

$$\begin{array}{r} 13 \\ - 6 \\ \hline \end{array}$$ $$\begin{array}{r} 6 \\ + 8 \\ \hline \end{array}$$ $$\begin{array}{r} 13 \\ - 9 \\ \hline \end{array}$$ $$\begin{array}{r} 14 \\ - 6 \\ \hline \end{array}$$ $$\begin{array}{r} 6 \\ + 6 \\ \hline \end{array}$$

$$\begin{array}{r} 4 \\ + 8 \\ \hline \end{array}$$ $$\begin{array}{r} 13 \\ - 4 \\ \hline \end{array}$$ $$\begin{array}{r} 14 \\ - 9 \\ \hline \end{array}$$ $$\begin{array}{r} 4 \\ + 9 \\ \hline \end{array}$$ $$\begin{array}{r} 13 \\ - 7 \\ \hline \end{array}$$

$$\begin{array}{r} 14 \\ - 7 \\ \hline \end{array}$$ $$\begin{array}{r} 6 \\ + 7 \\ \hline \end{array}$$ $$\begin{array}{r} 13 \\ - 5 \\ \hline \end{array}$$ $$\begin{array}{r} 5 \\ + 7 \\ \hline \end{array}$$

Mixed practice to 14

Pigs in Wigs

Name _____ Date _____

Read.

Write the math sentence.

There are 9 long wigs. There are 4 short wigs. How many wigs are there in all? _____ + _____ = _____	There are 14 pigs. 2 go home. How many pigs are left? _____ − _____ = _____
There are 13 wigs. 2 are curly. How many wigs are not curly? _____ − _____ = _____	There are 6 brushes. There are 8 combs. How many are there in all? _____ + _____ = _____
There are 12 wigs. The pigs try on 8. How many wigs did the pigs not try on? _____ − _____ = _____	7 wigs are black. 6 wigs are brown. How many wigs are there in all? _____ + _____ = _____
There are 8 short pigs. There are 4 tall pigs. How many pigs are there in all? _____ + _____ = _____	There are 13 wigs. The pigs buy 4. How many wigs are left? _____ − _____ = _____

Pretty As a Painting

Name _____   Date _____

Add and subtract.
Color by the code.

Color Code

7—orange   9—yellow
8—blue   14, 15, or 16—brown

Made in the Shade

Name _____   Date _____

Add and subtract.
Cross off a matching answer.

Answers

```
  16        14         7
-  8      -  6      +  9
____      ____      ____


   9        15         8        16        13
+  6      -  7      +  7      -  7      -  4
____      ____      ____      ____      ____


  15         8        14         6        15
-  8      +  8      -  5      +  9      -  9
____      ____      ____      ____      ____


   9        16         8        13         9
+  7      -  9      +  6      -  5      +  5
____      ____      ____      ____      ____


                                 8        13
                              +  5      -  9
                              ____      ____
```

Tree numbers: 8, 7, 4, 15, 9, 13, 14, 8, 9, 16, 8, 15, 16, 6, 9, 15, 16, 8, 7, 14

A "Bear-y" Fun Time!

Name _____ Date _____

Read.

Write the math sentence.

Bear catches 16 fish. He puts 9 back in the water. How many fish are left? ____ – ____ = ____	9 bears go swimming. 7 more bears go swimming. How many go swimming in all? ____ + ____ = ____
Bear has 6 fishing rods. He buys 9 more. How many fishing rods in all? ____ + ____ = ____	There are 15 headphones. Bear takes 8. How many headphones are left? ____ – ____ = ____

Bear reads 7 books.
He reads 8 more.
How many books does he
    read in all?
 	
____ + ____ = ____
	There are 14 inner tubes.
	8 pop.
	How many inner tubes are
	    left?
	
	____ – ____ = ____

Falling Numbers

Name _____   Date _____

Add or subtract.
Color by the code.

$$17 - 9$$

$$9 + 8$$

$$8 + 9$$

$$15 - 7$$

$$18 - 9$$

$$9 + 7$$

$$15 - 6$$

$$15 - 9$$

$$17 - 8$$

$$8 + 7$$

$$7 + 9$$

$$16 - 8$$

Color Code
6 or 7—red
8 or 9—yellow
14 or 15—green
16, 17, or 18—orange

$$15 - 8$$

$$9 + 9$$

$$16 - 9$$

$$16 - 7$$

$$8 + 8$$

$$9 + 5$$

Cool Character

Name _____   Date _____

Add or subtract.
Color by the code.

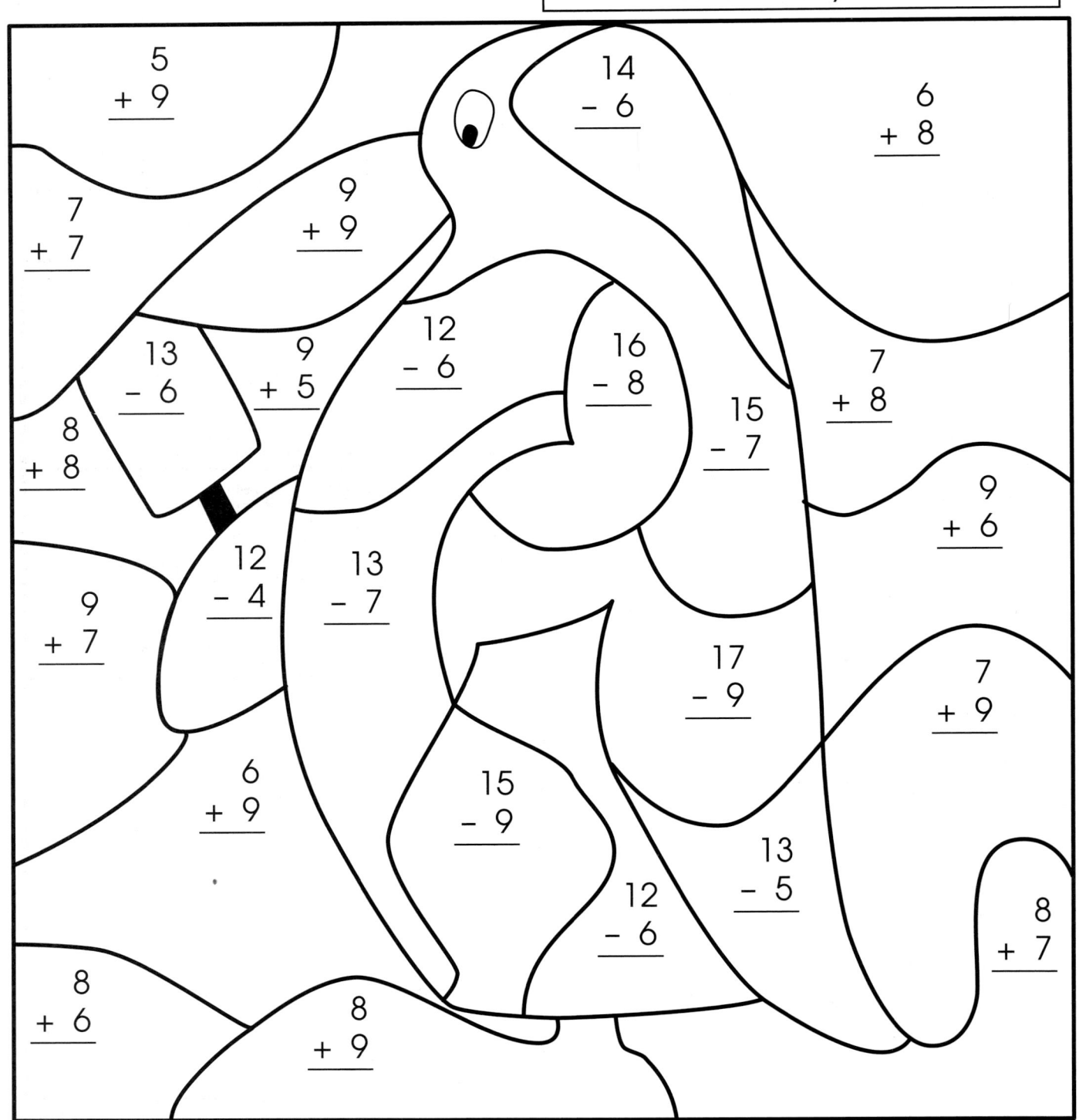

$$5 + 9$$

$$14 - 6$$

$$6 + 8$$

$$7 + 7$$

$$9 + 9$$

$$13 - 6$$

$$9 + 5$$

$$12 - 6$$

$$16 - 8$$

$$15 - 7$$

$$7 + 8$$

$$8 + 8$$

$$9 + 6$$

$$12 - 4$$

$$13 - 7$$

$$17 - 9$$

$$7 + 9$$

$$9 + 7$$

$$6 + 9$$

$$15 - 9$$

$$13 - 5$$

$$12 - 6$$

$$8 + 7$$

$$8 + 6$$

$$8 + 9$$

"Fix-o-saurus"

Name _____   Date _____

Dexter the dinosaur fixes cars.
Read.
Write the math sentence.

Dexter changes 9 tires. He changes 9 more. How many tires in all? _____ + _____ = _____	There are 17 cars. Dexter fixes 8. How many cars are left? _____ − _____ = _____
There are 16 windows. 7 break. How many windows are left? _____ − _____ = _____	Dexter has 18 tools. He loses 9. How many tools are left? _____ − _____ = _____
Dexter works for 8 hours. He works 9 more. How many hours in all? _____ + _____ = _____	7 cars are red. 9 cars are blue. How many cars in all? _____ + _____ = _____
There are 8 broken lights. There are 8 more lights. How many lights in all? _____ + _____ = _____	Dexter has 17 customers. 9 go home. How many customers are left? _____ − _____ = _____

Drive-In Dining

Name _____ Date _____

Read.
Write the math sentence.

There are 17 burgers.
The hippos eat 9.
How many burgers are left?

_____ − _____ = _____

There are 9 large drinks.
There are 7 small drinks.
How many drinks in all?

_____ + _____ = _____

The hippos make 16 shakes.
They sell 8.
How many shakes are left?

_____ − _____ = _____

There are 18 hippos.
9 go home.
How many hippos are left?

_____ − _____ = _____

The hippos make 9 hot dogs.
They make 9 more.
How many hot dogs in all?

_____ + _____ = _____

The hippos hear 7 songs.
They hear 8 more.
How many songs in all?

_____ + _____ = _____

There are 16 french fries.
The hippos eat 7.
How many french fries are
   left?

_____ − _____ = _____

There are 17 cars.
8 drive away.
How many cars are left?

_____ − _____ = _____

©The Education Center, Inc. • *Target Math Success* • TEC60826 • Key p. 136

Story problems: mixed practice to 18

Subtraction Strategies

Subtraction Strategies

Table of Contents

A Crunchy Carrot Crop

Name _____ Date _____

Count back 1.
Use the number line to help you.

10 − 1 = ___	6 − 1 = ___
8 − 1 = ___	2 − 1 = ___
1 − 1 = ___	7 − 1 = ___
4 − 1 = ___	5 − 1 = ___
9 − 1 = ___	3 − 1 = ___

©The Education Center, Inc. • Target Math Success • TEC60826 • Key p. 136

Monkeying Around the Playground

Name _____ Date _____

Count back 2.
Use the number line to help you.

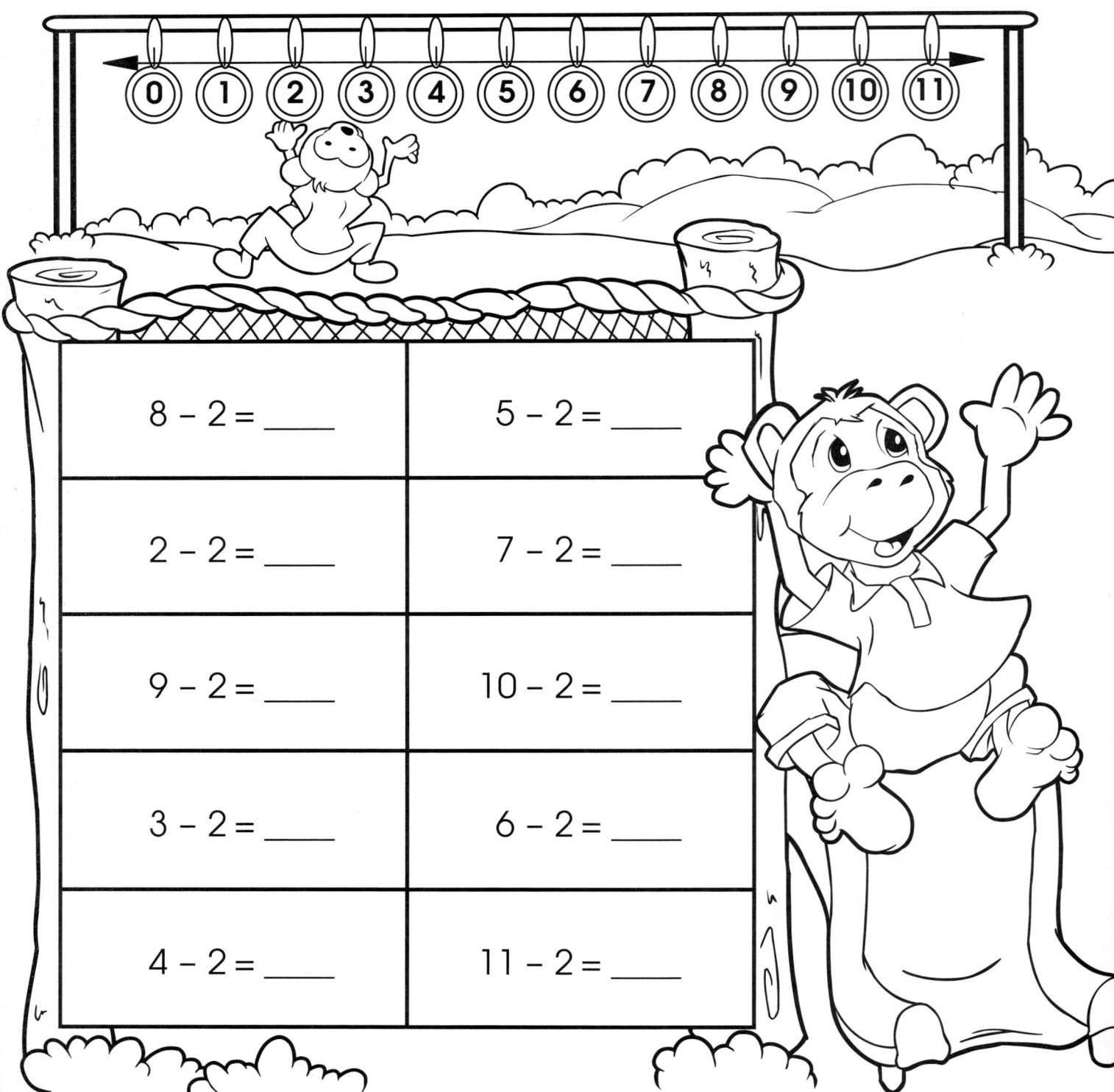

8 – 2 = ____	5 – 2 = ____
2 – 2 = ____	7 – 2 = ____
9 – 2 = ____	10 – 2 = ____
3 – 2 = ____	6 – 2 = ____
4 – 2 = ____	11 – 2 = ____

An "Apple-tizing" Snack

Name _____ Date _____

Count back 3.
Use the number line to help you.

9 – 3 = _____	3 – 3 = _____
12 – 3 = _____	7 – 3 = _____
4 – 3 = _____	10 – 3 = _____
8 – 3 = _____	6 – 3 = _____
11 – 3 = _____	5 – 3 = _____

Nuts About Numbers

Name _____   Date _____

Subtract.
Color by the code.

$$1 - 0$$

$$8 - 0$$

$$6 - 0$$

$$10 - 0$$

$$9 - 0$$

$$3 - 0$$

$$8 - 0$$

$$2 - 0$$

$$5 - 0$$

$$6 - 0$$

$$7 - 0$$

$$5 - 0$$

$$4 - 0$$

$$4 - 0$$

Sweet Treat

Name _____ Date _____

Subtract.
Color.

If a number is subtracted from itself, color the space **purple.**

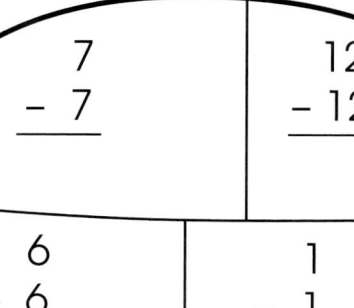

7 − 7	12 − 12		11 − 11	9 − 9
6 − 6	1 − 1		3 − 3	4 − 4
4 − 4	2 − 2	9 − 9	1 − 1	5 − 5	12 − 12
8 − 8	5 − 5	10 −10	2 − 2	7 − 7	6 − 6
11 − 11	3 − 3		10 − 10

It's Lunchtime

Name _____ Date _____

Subtract.
Add to check your answer.

$\begin{array}{r} 4 \\ -\ 1 \\ \hline 3 \end{array}$ $\begin{array}{r} 3 \\ +\ 1 \\ \hline 4 \end{array}$	$\begin{array}{r} 6 \\ -\ 2 \\ \hline \end{array}$ $+$
$\begin{array}{r} 8 \\ -\ 3 \\ \hline \end{array}$ $+$	$\begin{array}{r} 5 \\ -\ 4 \\ \hline \end{array}$ $+$
$\begin{array}{r} 7 \\ -\ 6 \\ \hline \end{array}$ $+$	$\begin{array}{r} 9 \\ -\ 6 \\ \hline \end{array}$ $+$
$\begin{array}{r} 10 \\ -\ 1 \\ \hline \end{array}$ $+$	$\begin{array}{r} 3 \\ -\ 2 \\ \hline \end{array}$ $+$
$\begin{array}{r} 5 \\ -\ 3 \\ \hline \end{array}$ $+$	$\begin{array}{r} 8 \\ -\ 2 \\ \hline \end{array}$ $+$

Using addition to check subtraction

Parent Communication and Student Checkups

Parent Communication and Student Checkups

Table of Contents

How to Administer the Checkups

Both checkups can be given at the same time, or Checkup B can be given as a follow-up test for students who did not do well on Checkup A. If desired, a time limit of **one minute** can be used when a test is given. This will help you determine which students have mastered a skill and which students may need more practice.

Student Progress Chart

_____ (student)		Date	Number Correct	Comments
Checkup 1: Subtraction facts to 5	A			
	B			
Checkup 2: Subtraction facts to 6	A			
	B			
Checkup 3: Subtraction facts to 7	A			
	B			
Checkup 4: Subtraction facts to 8	A			
	B			
Checkup 5: Subtraction facts to 9	A			
	B			
Checkup 6: Subtraction facts to 10	A			
	B			
Checkup 7: Subtraction facts to 11	A			
	B			
Checkup 8: Subtraction facts to 12	A			
	B			
Checkup 9: Subtraction facts to 14	A			
	B			
Checkup 10: Subtraction facts to 16	A			
	B			
Checkup 11: Subtraction facts to 18	A			
	B			

It's Time to Take Aim!

On _____ our class will be having a checkup on math facts. To help your child prepare, please spend about 15 minutes reviewing math problems that have **subtraction facts to 5.** Thanks for your help!

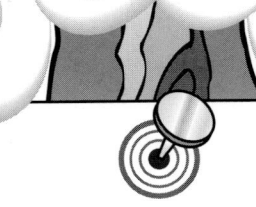

Target These!

1	2
1 – 0	2 – 0
1 – 1	2 – 1
	2 – 2

3	4
3 – 0	4 – 0
3 – 1	4 – 1
3 – 2	4 – 2
3 – 3	4 – 3
	4 – 4

5
5 – 0
5 – 1
5 – 2
5 – 3
5 – 4
5 – 5

4 pennies minus 1 penny
4 – 1 = 3

On-Target Practice

Heads or tails? It doesn't matter! Everyone wins with this fun activity! Give your child a pencil, a sheet of paper, and five pennies. Direct his attention to the differences between the heads side and the tails side of a penny. Then ask him to gently shake the coins between his hands and drop them on a carpeted surface. Next, have him write a math sentence based on what lands faceup. For example, if four coins land on heads and one coin lands on tails, he should write "4 – 1 = 3". Then have him scoop up the pennies, give them a shake, and drop them again. Repeat this activity several times. Now that's right on the money!

If your child is quick to know the answers to these math problems, an occasional review may be all he or she needs. But if some of the answers come more slowly, it's a good idea to spend a few minutes each day having your child work with math facts at home.

Checkup 1

Name _____   Date _____

A. $\begin{array}{r} 5 \\ -0 \\ \hline \end{array}$ $\begin{array}{r} 4 \\ -1 \\ \hline \end{array}$ $\begin{array}{r} 1 \\ -0 \\ \hline \end{array}$ $\begin{array}{r} 3 \\ -2 \\ \hline \end{array}$ $\begin{array}{r} 4 \\ -4 \\ \hline \end{array}$

B. $\begin{array}{r} 2 \\ -1 \\ \hline \end{array}$ $\begin{array}{r} 5 \\ -2 \\ \hline \end{array}$ $\begin{array}{r} 4 \\ -2 \\ \hline \end{array}$ $\begin{array}{r} 5 \\ -4 \\ \hline \end{array}$ $\begin{array}{r} 3 \\ -0 \\ \hline \end{array}$

C. $\begin{array}{r} 5 \\ -3 \\ \hline \end{array}$ $\begin{array}{r} 2 \\ -2 \\ \hline \end{array}$ $\begin{array}{r} 3 \\ -1 \\ \hline \end{array}$ $\begin{array}{r} 5 \\ -1 \\ \hline \end{array}$ $\begin{array}{r} 3 \\ -3 \\ \hline \end{array}$

D. $\begin{array}{r} 1 \\ -1 \\ \hline \end{array}$ $\begin{array}{r} 2 \\ -0 \\ \hline \end{array}$ $\begin{array}{r} 4 \\ -3 \\ \hline \end{array}$ $\begin{array}{r} 5 \\ -5 \\ \hline \end{array}$ $\begin{array}{r} 4 \\ -0 \\ \hline \end{array}$

E. $\begin{array}{r} 3 \\ -2 \\ \hline \end{array}$ $\begin{array}{r} 2 \\ -1 \\ \hline \end{array}$ $\begin{array}{r} 5 \\ -0 \\ \hline \end{array}$ $\begin{array}{r} 4 \\ -4 \\ \hline \end{array}$ $\begin{array}{r} 1 \\ -0 \\ \hline \end{array}$

Test A: Subtraction facts to 5

©The Education Center, Inc. • *Target Math Success* • TEC60826 • Key: inside back cover

105

Checkup 1

Name _____   Date _____

A. $\begin{array}{r} 3 \\ -0 \\ \hline \end{array}$ $\begin{array}{r} 2 \\ -2 \\ \hline \end{array}$ $\begin{array}{r} 4 \\ -3 \\ \hline \end{array}$ $\begin{array}{r} 2 \\ -0 \\ \hline \end{array}$ $\begin{array}{r} 3 \\ -2 \\ \hline \end{array}$

B. $\begin{array}{r} 5 \\ -2 \\ \hline \end{array}$ $\begin{array}{r} 4 \\ -4 \\ \hline \end{array}$ $\begin{array}{r} 5 \\ -0 \\ \hline \end{array}$ $\begin{array}{r} 1 \\ -0 \\ \hline \end{array}$ $\begin{array}{r} 4 \\ -2 \\ \hline \end{array}$

C. $\begin{array}{r} 3 \\ -1 \\ \hline \end{array}$ $\begin{array}{r} 5 \\ -0 \\ \hline \end{array}$ $\begin{array}{r} 2 \\ -2 \\ \hline \end{array}$ $\begin{array}{r} 5 \\ -3 \\ \hline \end{array}$ $\begin{array}{r} 2 \\ -0 \\ \hline \end{array}$

D. $\begin{array}{r} 4 \\ -1 \\ \hline \end{array}$ $\begin{array}{r} 2 \\ -1 \\ \hline \end{array}$ $\begin{array}{r} 5 \\ -4 \\ \hline \end{array}$ $\begin{array}{r} 1 \\ -1 \\ \hline \end{array}$ $\begin{array}{r} 3 \\ -3 \\ \hline \end{array}$

E. $\begin{array}{r} 2 \\ -0 \\ \hline \end{array}$ $\begin{array}{r} 5 \\ -3 \\ \hline \end{array}$ $\begin{array}{r} 4 \\ -0 \\ \hline \end{array}$ $\begin{array}{r} 3 \\ -2 \\ \hline \end{array}$ $\begin{array}{r} 1 \\ -0 \\ \hline \end{array}$

Test B: Subtraction facts to 5

©The Education Center, Inc. • *Target Math Success* • TEC60826 • Key: inside back cover

It's Time to Take Aim!

On _____ our class will be having a checkup on math facts. To help your child prepare, please spend about 15 minutes reviewing **subtraction facts to 6.** Thanks for your help!

Target These!

1	2
0 – 1	2 – 0
1 – 0	2 – 1
	2 – 2

3	4
3 – 0	4 – 0
3 – 1	4 – 1
3 – 2	4 – 2
3 – 3	4 – 3
	4 – 4

5
5 – 0
5 – 1
5 – 2
5 – 3
5 – 4
5 – 5

6
6 – 0
6 – 1
6 – 2
6 – 3
6 – 4
6 – 5
6 – 6

On-Target Practice

Pull out those family photographs and get ready for subtraction practice. With the help of your child, select six family photographs and place each one in a different resealable plastic bag (to protect the photographs). Ask your youngster to lay the six photographs in a row. Call out a subtraction fact for six, such as 6 – 1, and have your child represent this fact using the photographs as counters. Then ask your child to state the math fact (6 – 1 = 5). After calling out the remaining facts for six, repeat this activity several more times, using facts for five, four, and three. (Be sure to adjust the number of photographs used to match the math fact.) What a great family activity!

6 photographs minus 1 photograph.
6 - 1 = 5

     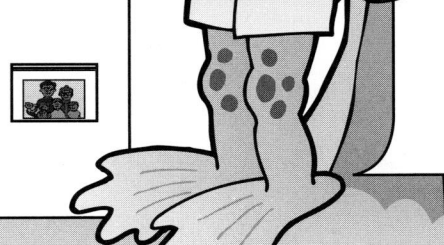

If your child is quick to know the answers to these math problems, an occasional review may be all he or she needs. But if some of the answers come more slowly, it's a good idea to spend a few minutes each day having your child work with math facts at home.

©The Education Center, Inc. • *Target Math Success* • TEC60826

106

Checkup 2

Name _____   Date _____

A. 6 5 6 5 5
   −1 −0 −6 −4 −1

B. 4 5 2 6 4
   −2 −5 −1 −0 −4

C. 3 6 4 3 6
   −3 −2 −3 −0 −5

D. 5 4 3 6 5
   −3 −1 −2 −3 −2

E. 6 5 3 4 2
   −2 −4 −1 −2 −2

Test A: Subtraction facts to 6

Checkup 2

Name _____   Date _____

A. 5 6 5 4 6
   −5 −4 −2 −4 −0

B. 4 6 2 3 5
   −1 −6 −2 −0 −1

C. 4 4 4 5 6
   −3 −2 −0 −4 −1

D. 6 3 3 6 5
   −2 −2 −1 −3 −0

E. 2 5 4 6 3
   −0 −3 −4 −5 −3

Test B: Subtraction facts to 6

It's Time to Take Aim!

On _____ our class will be having a checkup on math facts. To help your child prepare, please spend about 15 minutes reviewing **subtraction facts to 7.** Thanks for your help!

I know the opposite side of the die says 3 because **7 - 4 = 3**

On-Target Practice

Get your child rolling through subtraction! To begin, give your child a sheet of paper, a pencil, and one die. Tell him that the numbers on the opposite sides of a die add up to seven. Direct him to roll the die and determine the number on the other side of the die. To do this, have him announce the number he rolls (4 for example) and subtract it from seven. Ask him to write the subtraction problem on his paper and complete the math fact (7 – 4 = 3). Then have him lift the die to check his answer. No doubt your child will give this activity two thumbs-up!

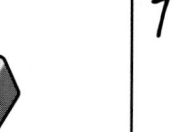

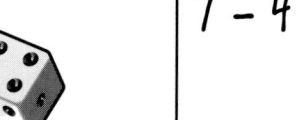

$$7 - 4 = 3$$

Target These!

1	2	3
0 – 1	2 – 0	3 – 0
1 – 0	2 – 1	3 – 1
	2 – 2	3 – 2
		3 – 3

4	5	6
4 – 0	5 – 0	6 – 0
4 – 1	5 – 1	6 – 1
4 – 2	5 – 2	6 – 2
4 – 3	5 – 3	6 – 3
4 – 4	5 – 4	6 – 4
	5 – 5	6 – 5
		6 – 6

7
7 – 0
7 – 1
7 – 2
7 – 3
7 – 4
7 – 5
7 – 6
7 – 7

If your child is quick to know the answers to these math problems, an occasional review may be all he or she needs. But if some of the answers come more slowly, it's a good idea to spend a few minutes each day having your child work with math facts at home.

Checkup 3

Name _____   Date _____

A. 7   5   7   6
   − 0   − 2   − 2   − 4

B. 6   7   6   7
   − 1   − 4   − 3   − 7

C. 7   6   7   6
   − 6   − 0   − 1   − 2

D. 5   7   5   7
   − 0   − 3   − 1   − 5

E. 7   5   6   4
   − 2   − 4   − 5   − 2

Checkup 3

Name _____   Date _____

A. 7   5   5   7
   − 1   − 0   − 2   − 3

B. 6   7   6   6
   − 6   − 0   − 2   − 5

C. 7   6   5   7
   − 7   − 1   − 4   − 2

D. 6   7   6   6
   − 3   − 4   − 0   − 4

E. 6   2   4   5
   − 5   − 2   − 2   − 3

It's Time to Take Aim!

On _____ our class will be having a checkup on math facts. To help your child prepare, please spend about 15 minutes reviewing **subtraction facts to 8.** Thanks for your help!

On-Target Practice

Help your child practice subtraction facts in a snap with this idea! Ask your child to turn a chair around and sit facing the back of it. Then have him clip eight clothespins to the back of the chair. Announce a subtraction problem that begins with eight and have your child remove clothespins to show the answer. Continue in this same manner with a new fact. For further practice, remove a clothespin and have your child repeat the activity reviewing subtraction facts beginning with seven!

8 clothespins minus 4 clothespins
$8 - 4 = 4$

Target These!

1	2	3
$1 - 0$	$2 - 0$	$3 - 0$
$1 - 1$	$2 - 1$	$3 - 1$
	$2 - 2$	$3 - 2$
		$3 - 3$

4	5	6
$4 - 0$	$5 - 0$	$6 - 0$
$4 - 1$	$5 - 1$	$6 - 1$
$4 - 2$	$5 - 2$	$6 - 2$
$4 - 3$	$5 - 3$	$6 - 3$
$4 - 4$	$5 - 4$	$6 - 4$
	$5 - 5$	$6 - 5$
		$6 - 6$

7	8
$7 - 0$	$8 - 0$
$7 - 1$	$8 - 1$
$7 - 2$	$8 - 2$
$7 - 3$	$8 - 3$
$7 - 4$	$8 - 4$
$7 - 5$	$8 - 5$
$7 - 6$	$8 - 6$
$7 - 7$	$8 - 7$
	$8 - 8$

If your child is quick to know the answers to these math problems, an occasional review may be all he or she needs. But if some of the answers come more slowly, it's a good idea to spend a few minutes each day having your child work with math facts at home.

110

Checkup 4

A. 5 − 3   4 − 1   7 − 2   8 − 5   6 − 4

B. 7 − 3   4 − 0   7 − 6   8 − 3   6 − 6

C. 8 − 7   6 − 1   5 − 2   7 − 7   8 − 4

D. 6 − 3   5 − 1   8 − 2   8 − 6   7 − 4

E. 4 − 3   3 − 2   2 − 2   5 − 0   4 − 2

Test A: Subtraction facts to 8

Checkup 4

A. 8 − 0   6 − 2   5 − 4   6 − 0   4 − 2

B. 7 − 1   4 − 3   8 − 5   7 − 5   6 − 5

C. 8 − 7   7 − 0   8 − 1   6 − 3   8 − 4

D. 7 − 3   8 − 8   6 − 2   5 − 5   8 − 6

E. 5 − 3   2 − 0   3 − 2   4 − 1   3 − 3

Test B: Subtraction facts to 8

It's Time to Take Aim!

On _____ our class will be having a checkup on math facts. To help your child prepare, please spend about 15 minutes reviewing **subtraction facts to 9.** Thanks for your help!

9 – 6 = 3

Target These!

3	4	5
3 – 0	4 – 0	5 – 0
3 – 1	4 – 1	5 – 1
3 – 2	4 – 2	5 – 2
3 – 3	4 – 3	5 – 3
	4 – 4	5 – 4
		5 – 5

6	7
6 – 0	7 – 0
6 – 1	7 – 1
6 – 2	7 – 2
6 – 3	7 – 3
6 – 4	7 – 4
6 – 5	7 – 5
6 – 6	7 – 6
	7 – 7

8	9
8 – 0	9 – 0
8 – 1	9 – 1
8 – 2	9 – 2
8 – 3	9 – 3
8 – 4	9 – 4
8 – 5	9 – 5
8 – 6	9 – 6
8 – 7	9 – 7
8 – 8	9 – 8
	9 – 9

On-Target Practice

Staying on target with subtraction facts is in the cards with this hands-on activity! To prepare, remove the tens, jacks, queens, and kings from a regular deck of cards. Remove a nine card from the deck and place it on a table. Shuffle the remaining cards and give them to your child. Have him flip over a card and lay it below the nine. Next, ask him to say the subtraction math sentence the cards represent and then give the answer. (An ace represents 1.) After confirming the answer, have him place the card in a discard pile and continue in the same manner until all of the cards have been subtracted from nine. For more practice, remove the nines from the deck. Place an eight card on the table, reshuffle the remaining cards, and repeat this activity with differences through eight.

If your child is quick to know the answers to these math problems, an occasional review may be all he or she needs. But if some of the answers come more slowly, it's a good idea to spend a few minutes each day having your child work with math facts at home.

Checkup 5

Checkup 5

Name _____ Date _____

Name _____ Date _____

Test A (left)

A. 8 − 3   7 − 2   9 − 5   9 − 1

B. 5 − 3   6 − 4   7 − 0   8 − 6

C. 9 − 2   6 − 2   9 − 8   5 − 4

D. 8 − 5   9 − 3   7 − 6   9 − 7

E. 6 − 5   5 − 4   5 − 3   3 − 2

Test A: Subtraction facts to 9

©The Education Center, Inc. • *Target Math Success* • TEC60826 • Key: inside back cover

Test B (right)

A. 7 − 1   9 − 4   8 − 4   9 − 9

B. 9 − 6   8 − 8   7 − 4   9 − 0

C. 9 − 8   8 − 0   6 − 2   7 − 5

D. 7 − 7   6 − 5   9 − 3   8 − 1

E. 5 − 3   3 − 3   5 − 2   4 − 2

Test B: Subtraction facts to 9

©The Education Center, Inc. • *Target Math Success* • TEC60826 • Key: inside back cover

It's Time to Take Aim!

On _____ our class will be having a checkup on math facts. To help your child prepare, please spend about 15 minutes reviewing **subtraction facts to 10.** Thanks for your help!

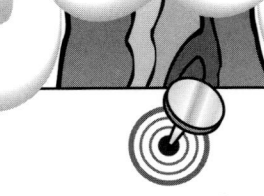

Target These!

4	5	6
4 – 0	5 – 0	6 – 0
4 – 1	5 – 1	6 – 1
4 – 2	5 – 2	6 – 2
4 – 3	5 – 3	6 – 3
4 – 4	5 – 4	6 – 4
	5 – 5	6 – 5
		6 – 6

7	8
7 – 0	8 – 0
7 – 1	8 – 1
7 – 2	8 – 2
7 – 3	8 – 3
7 – 4	8 – 4
7 – 5	8 – 5
7 – 6	8 – 6
7 – 7	8 – 7
	8 – 8

9	10
9 – 0	10 – 0
9 – 1	10 – 1
9 – 2	10 – 2
9 – 3	10 – 3
9 – 4	10 – 4
9 – 5	10 – 5
9 – 6	10 – 6
9 – 7	10 – 7
9 – 8	10 – 8
9 – 9	10 – 9
	10 – 10

> 10 bottle caps minus 6 bottle caps
> **10 – 6 = 4**

On-Target Practice

This fun math game provides great fact practice for your child! Using basic subtraction facts to ten, write a different fact on one index card and its answer on a separate card. Next, place the fact cards facedown in random order. Repeat this step with the answer cards, placing them in a separate area near the fact cards. Then have your youngster turn over a card from each area. If he draws a matching fact and answer, he keeps the cards and continues play. (As needed, encourage your child to use small items such as plastic bottle caps or pasta pieces to determine the answer.) If the cards do not match, he returns them facedown to their original places. Continue play until all cards have been matched. For additional practice, remove two fact cards and their matching answer cards and replace them with more cards for nine. Repeat this step with two fact and answer cards each for eight, seven, and six.

If your child is quick to know the answers to these math problems, an occasional review may be all he or she needs. But if some of the answers come more slowly, it's a good idea to spend a few minutes each day having your child work with math facts at home.

Checkup 6

Name _____   Date _____

A. 10   9   8   10   9
   − 0 − 4 − 5 − 7 − 3

B.   9 10   8   10   9
   − 5 − 8 − 6 − 3 − 1

C.   7 10   9   8   10
   − 5 − 4 − 7 − 2 − 1

D. 10 10   9   8   10
   − 6 − 2 − 8 − 3 − 9

E.   7 10   8   9   10
   − 3 −10 − 4 − 6 − 5

©The Education Center, Inc. • Target Math Success • TEC60826 • Key: inside back cover

Test A: Subtraction facts to 10

Checkup 6

Name _____   Date _____

A.   9 10   9   10   10
   − 1 − 5 − 4 − 1 − 7

B. 10   9   8   9   10
   − 2 − 3 − 2 − 8 − 6

C.   9 10   8   10   9
   − 7 − 8 − 7 − 3 − 5

D.   9 10   8   7   10
   − 6 − 4 − 3 − 5 − 0

E.   8 10   7   10   8
   − 5 − 9 − 4 −10 − 4

©The Education Center, Inc. • Target Math Success • TEC60826 • Key: inside back cover

Test B: Subtraction facts to 10

It's Time to Take Aim!

On _____ our class will be having a checkup on math facts. To help your child prepare, please spend about 15 minutes reviewing **subtraction facts to 11.** Thanks for your help!

On-Target Practice

A disposable dinner plate divided into two sections is an easy-to-use tool for practicing subtraction facts. Draw a line down the plate to show the left side larger. After the two sections are drawn, place 11 pieces of popcorn into the larger section. Then call out a fact for 11 from the list shown at the right. For example, call out 11 – 4. Have your child move four popcorn pieces to the right side of the plate. Then have him count the remaining pieces on the left side. Ask your child to restate the subtraction fact to include the answer (11 – 4 = 7). After confirming his answer, move the popcorn pieces back to the left side of the plate and continue in this same manner with the remaining facts for 11. Then top off the activity by inviting your child to munch on his popcorn!

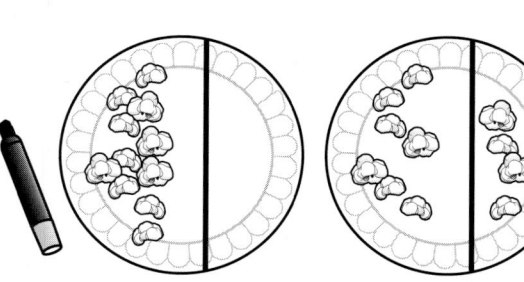

11 popcorn pieces minus 4 popcorn pieces
11 – 4 = 7

Target These!

5	6	7
5 – 0	6 – 0	7 – 0
5 – 1	6 – 1	7 – 1
5 – 2	6 – 2	7 – 2
5 – 3	6 – 3	7 – 3
5 – 4	6 – 4	7 – 4
5 – 5	6 – 5	7 – 5
	6 – 6	7 – 6
		7 – 7

8	9
8 – 0	9 – 0
8 – 1	9 – 1
8 – 2	9 – 2
8 – 3	9 – 3
8 – 4	9 – 4
8 – 5	9 – 5
8 – 6	9 – 6
8 – 7	9 – 7
8 – 8	9 – 8
	9 – 9

10	11
10 – 0	11 – 0
10 – 1	11 – 1
10 – 2	11 – 2
10 – 3	11 – 3
10 – 4	11 – 4
10 – 5	11 – 5
10 – 6	11 – 6
10 – 7	11 – 7
10 – 8	11 – 8
10 – 9	11 – 9
10 – 10	11 – 10
	11 – 11

If your child is quick to know the answers to these math problems, an occasional review may be all he or she needs. But if some of the answers come more slowly, it's a good idea to spend a few minutes each day having your child work with math facts at home.

Checkup 7

Name _____ Date _____

A.

10	11	9	10
− 3	− 9	− 7	− 8

B.

11	10	10	9
− 4	− 7	− 2	− 4

C.

11	10	7	11
− 5	− 4	− 4	− 3

D.

9	10	11	8
− 7	− 1	− 7	− 2

E.

11	10	8	11
− 6	− 10	− 5	− 2

Test A: Subtraction facts to 11

©The Education Center, Inc. • *Target Math Success* • TEC60826 • Key: inside back cover

Checkup 7

Name _____ Date _____

A.

11	9	10	11	9
− 8	− 5	− 3	− 4	− 7

B.

10	11	10	11	10
− 9	− 5	− 2	− 9	− 5

C.

10	11	9	10	10
− 0	− 7	− 3	− 7	− 4

D.

11	9	10	8	11
− 3	− 6	− 1	− 2	− 6

E.

10	8	11	7	8
− 8	− 5	− 2	− 3	− 0

Test B: Subtraction facts to 11

©The Education Center, Inc. • *Target Math Success* • TEC60826 • Key: inside back cover

It's Time to Take Aim!

On _____ our class will be having a checkup on math facts. To help your child prepare, please spend about 15 minutes reviewing **subtraction facts to 12.** Thanks for your help!

On-Target Practice

Stick with this idea to provide plenty of subtraction practice for your child! Number seven small squares of paper from 3 to 9 and stack them facedown on a table. Also place nine cotton balls on the table. Next, attach 12 stickers to a sheet of paper. To begin, ask your child to draw a card from the stack and say the subtraction sentence represented by the stickers and the card. For example, if he drew the card labeled "6", he would say, "Twelve minus six." Then have him use the cotton balls to cover the corresponding number of items and give the answer. After confirming his answer, have him place the card in a discard pile and remove the cotton balls. Then have him repeat the activity with the remaining cards.

12 - 6 = 6

Target These!

6	7	8
6 − 0	7 − 0	8 − 0
6 − 1	7 − 1	8 − 1
6 − 2	7 − 2	8 − 2
6 − 3	7 − 3	8 − 3
6 − 4	7 − 4	8 − 4
6 − 5	7 − 5	8 − 5
6 − 6	7 − 6	8 − 6
	7 − 7	8 − 7
		8 − 8

9	10
9 − 0	10 − 0
9 − 1	10 − 1
9 − 2	10 − 2
9 − 3	10 − 3
9 − 4	10 − 4
9 − 5	10 − 5
9 − 6	10 − 6
9 − 7	10 − 7
9 − 8	10 − 8
9 − 9	10 − 9
	10 − 10

11	12
11 − 2	12 − 3
11 − 3	12 − 4
11 − 4	12 − 5
11 − 5	12 − 6
11 − 6	12 − 7
11 − 7	12 − 8
11 − 8	12 − 9
11 − 9	

If your child is quick to know the answers to these math problems, an occasional review may be all he or she needs. But if some of the answers come more slowly, it's a good idea to spend a few minutes each day having your child work with math facts at home.

Checkup 8

Name _____ Date _____

A.
$$11 - 9$$ $$10 - 7$$ $$9 - 8$$ $$12 - 5$$ $$9 - 4$$

B.
$$10 - 6$$ $$11 - 4$$ $$9 - 7$$ $$11 - 3$$ $$10 - 8$$

C.
$$12 - 9$$ $$11 - 7$$ $$12 - 6$$ $$9 - 5$$ $$10 - 3$$

D.
$$11 - 5$$ $$12 - 8$$ $$10 - 9$$ $$9 - 2$$ $$12 - 3$$

E.
$$11 - 2$$ $$12 - 7$$ $$10 - 5$$ $$11 - 8$$ $$12 - 4$$

Test A: Subtraction facts to 12

©The Education Center, Inc. • *Target Math Success* • TEC60826 • Key: inside back cover

Checkup 8

Name _____ Date _____

A.
$$11 - 6$$ $$9 - 6$$ $$10 - 1$$ $$9 - 1$$ $$12 - 5$$

B.
$$9 - 3$$ $$10 - 4$$ $$12 - 4$$ $$11 - 5$$ $$9 - 9$$

C.
$$10 - 2$$ $$11 - 9$$ $$10 - 5$$ $$9 - 7$$ $$12 - 8$$

D.
$$12 - 4$$ $$11 - 4$$ $$12 - 3$$ $$11 - 9$$ $$10 - 8$$

E.
$$11 - 2$$ $$10 - 0$$ $$12 - 6$$ $$12 - 7$$ $$10 - 10$$

Test B: Subtraction facts to 12

©The Education Center, Inc. • *Target Math Success* • TEC60826 • Key: inside back cover

It's Time to Take Aim!

On _____ our class will be having a checkup on math facts. To help your child prepare, please spend about 15 minutes reviewing **subtraction facts to 14.** Thanks for your help!

14 - 6 = 8

Target These!

8	9	10
8 – 0	9 – 0	10 – 0
8 – 1	9 – 1	10 – 1
8 – 2	9 – 2	10 – 2
8 – 3	9 – 3	10 – 3
8 – 4	9 – 4	10 – 4
8 – 5	9 – 5	10 – 5
8 – 6	9 – 6	10 – 6
8 – 7	9 – 7	10 – 7
8 – 8	9 – 8	10 – 8
	9 – 9	10 – 9
		10 – 10

11	12
11 – 2	12 – 3
11 – 3	12 – 4
11 – 4	12 – 5
11 – 5	12 – 6
11 – 6	12 – 7
11 – 7	12 – 8
11 – 8	12 – 9
11 – 9	

13	14
13 – 4	14 – 5
13 – 5	14 – 6
13 – 6	14 – 7
13 – 7	14 – 8
13 – 8	14 – 9
13 – 9	

On-Target Practice

This easy-to-create pasta board is the perfect tool for keeping your child's subtraction skills on target! To create a board, string 14 pasta pieces (such as penne or wagon wheels) onto a length of yarn. Holding the yarn taut, tape each end to a tabletop and slide the pasta pieces to the left. To begin the activity, say a math fact from the list. Ask your child to slide the corresponding number of pasta pieces to the right. Then have him separate the pasta to show the math fact. The answer will be the remaining number of pasta pieces on the right side of the yarn. Then have him write the complete math sentence on a sheet of paper. Continue in this same manner for each remaining fact. Oh, the "pasta-bilities"!

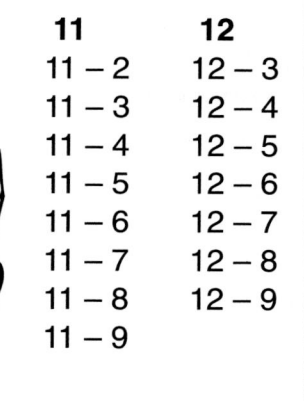

If your child is quick to know the answers to these math problems, an occasional review may be all he or she needs. But if some of the answers come more slowly, it's a good idea to spend a few minutes each day having your child work with math facts at home.

Checkup 9

Name _____

Date _____

A.
$$10 - 8$$
$$11 - 5$$
$$12 - 7$$
$$13 - 9$$
$$12 - 4$$

B.
$$12 - 6$$
$$10 - 5$$
$$11 - 3$$
$$12 - 9$$
$$13 - 4$$

C.
$$14 - 7$$
$$13 - 6$$
$$11 - 7$$
$$14 - 5$$
$$13 - 8$$

D.
$$11 - 2$$
$$12 - 3$$
$$13 - 5$$
$$14 - 9$$
$$11 - 4$$

E.
$$13 - 7$$
$$14 - 8$$
$$11 - 9$$
$$14 - 6$$
$$10 - 9$$

Checkup 9

Name _____

Date _____

A.
$$11 - 6$$
$$12 - 5$$
$$11 - 8$$
$$10 - 6$$
$$11 - 4$$

B.
$$12 - 8$$
$$10 - 7$$
$$13 - 9$$
$$14 - 7$$
$$13 - 7$$

C.
$$14 - 6$$
$$13 - 6$$
$$12 - 3$$
$$10 - 4$$
$$12 - 6$$

D.
$$13 - 5$$
$$11 - 2$$
$$14 - 9$$
$$13 - 4$$
$$12 - 8$$

E.
$$14 - 5$$
$$12 - 7$$
$$11 - 8$$
$$12 - 9$$
$$14 - 8$$

It's Time to Take Aim!

On _____ our class will be having a checkup on math facts. To help your child prepare, please spend about 15 minutes reviewing **subtraction facts to 16.** Thanks for your help!

On-Target Practice

Here's a cozy way to review basic subtraction facts. Lay your child's favorite pullover sweater or jacket on a flat surface next to a bowl of 16 buttons. Lay a length of string or yarn down the middle of the sweater to divide it into two sections. Tell your youngster to arrange the 16 buttons on the left half of the sweater. Then call out a math fact for 16, such as 16 – 9. Have your youngster represent the fact by moving the correct number of buttons to the other side of the sweater *(9)*. Then have her count the remaining buttons on the left side and say the problem as a number sentence *(16 – 9 = 7)*. After confirming her answer, have her return the nine buttons to the left side of the sweater. For additional practice, remove a button and practice subtraction facts to 15.

> 16 buttons minus 9 buttons.
> **16 - 9 = 7**

Target These!

10	11	12
10 – 0	11 – 2	12 – 3
10 – 1	11 – 3	12 – 4
10 – 2	11 – 4	12 – 5
10 – 3	11 – 5	12 – 6
10 – 4	11 – 6	12 – 7
10 – 5	11 – 7	12 – 8
10 – 6	11 – 8	12 – 9
10 – 7	11 – 9	
10 – 8		
10 – 9		
10 – 10		

13	14	15
13 – 4	14 – 5	15 – 6
13 – 5	14 – 6	15 – 7
13 – 6	14 – 7	15 – 8
13 – 7	14 – 8	15 – 9
13 – 8	14 – 9	
13 – 9		

16
16 – 7
16 – 8
16 – 9

If your child is quick to know the answers to these math problems, an occasional review may be all he or she needs. But if some of the answers come more slowly, it's a good idea to spend a few minutes each day having your child work with math facts at home.

Checkup 10

Name _____ Date _____

A. 16   12   13
   − 8   − 7   − 8

B. 12   13   14
   − 4   − 6   − 9

C. 14   16   13
   − 6   − 7   − 7

D. 12   13   14
   − 3   − 5   − 8

E. 14   12   11
   − 7   − 9   − 4

Test A: Subtraction facts to 16

©The Education Center, Inc. • *Target Math Success* • TEC60826 • Key: inside back cover

123

Checkup 10

Name _____ Date _____

A. 16   13   12   14
   − 7   − 6   − 3   − 5

B. 12   15   13   15
   − 7   − 6   − 4   − 7

C. 15   14   16   13
   − 8   − 6   − 9   − 7

D. 16   14   12   12
   − 8   − 7   − 5   − 9

E. 14   13   12   15
   − 8   − 5   − 4   − 9

Test B: Subtraction facts to 16

©The Education Center, Inc. • *Target Math Success* • TEC60826 • Key: inside back cover

It's Time to Take Aim!

On _____ our class will be having a checkup on math facts. To help your child prepare, please spend about 15 minutes reviewing **subtraction facts to 18.** Thanks for your help!

Target These!

12	13
12 − 3	13 − 4
12 − 4	13 − 5
12 − 5	13 − 6
12 − 6	13 − 7
12 − 7	13 − 8
12 − 8	13 − 9
12 − 9	

14	15
14 − 5	15 − 6
14 − 6	15 − 7
14 − 7	15 − 8
14 − 8	15 − 9
14 − 9	

16
16 − 7
16 − 8
16 − 9

17	18
17 − 8	18 − 9
17 − 9	

On-Target Practice

Two hats and 18 small blocks (or similar small objects) make subtraction practice hands-on fun! Place the hats side by side and then put 18 blocks inside one hat. Call out a math fact for 18, such as 18 − 9. Tell your youngster to remove nine blocks and place them inside the empty hat. Then have him count the remaining blocks in the first hat. After he determines the answer, have him say the math fact as a number sentence *(18 − 9 = 9)*. To repeat this activity with subtraction facts to 17, set aside one block and place the remaining blocks inside one hat. Then call out the math facts. For additional practice, remove another block and practice math facts to 16. Now that's using your noggin!

> 18 blocks minus 9 blocks.
> **18 − 9 = 9**

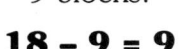

 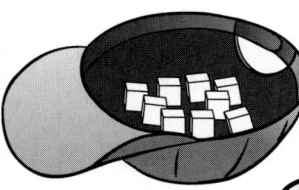

If your child is quick to know the answers to these math problems, an occasional review may be all he or she needs. But if some of the answers come more slowly, it's a good idea to spend a few minutes each day having your child work with math facts at home.

Checkup 11

Name _____   Date _____

A.	$\begin{array}{r} 18 \\ -\ 9 \\ \hline \end{array}$	$\begin{array}{r} 13 \\ -\ 9 \\ \hline \end{array}$	$\begin{array}{r} 15 \\ -\ 6 \\ \hline \end{array}$	$\begin{array}{r} 16 \\ -\ 9 \\ \hline \end{array}$	$\begin{array}{r} 14 \\ -\ 8 \\ \hline \end{array}$
B.	$\begin{array}{r} 13 \\ -\ 6 \\ \hline \end{array}$	$\begin{array}{r} 15 \\ -\ 9 \\ \hline \end{array}$	$\begin{array}{r} 12 \\ -\ 5 \\ \hline \end{array}$	$\begin{array}{r} 13 \\ -\ 8 \\ \hline \end{array}$	$\begin{array}{r} 12 \\ -\ 3 \\ \hline \end{array}$
C.	$\begin{array}{r} 16 \\ -\ 8 \\ \hline \end{array}$	$\begin{array}{r} 14 \\ -\ 7 \\ \hline \end{array}$	$\begin{array}{r} 17 \\ -\ 9 \\ \hline \end{array}$	$\begin{array}{r} 12 \\ -\ 7 \\ \hline \end{array}$	$\begin{array}{r} 16 \\ -\ 7 \\ \hline \end{array}$
D.	$\begin{array}{r} 14 \\ -\ 6 \\ \hline \end{array}$	$\begin{array}{r} 15 \\ -\ 8 \\ \hline \end{array}$	$\begin{array}{r} 13 \\ -\ 7 \\ \hline \end{array}$	$\begin{array}{r} 13 \\ -\ 5 \\ \hline \end{array}$	$\begin{array}{r} 14 \\ -\ 9 \\ \hline \end{array}$
E.	$\begin{array}{r} 17 \\ -\ 8 \\ \hline \end{array}$	$\begin{array}{r} 12 \\ -\ 8 \\ \hline \end{array}$	$\begin{array}{r} 14 \\ -\ 5 \\ \hline \end{array}$	$\begin{array}{r} 13 \\ -\ 4 \\ \hline \end{array}$	$\begin{array}{r} 15 \\ -\ 7 \\ \hline \end{array}$

Test A: Subtraction facts to 18

©The Education Center, Inc. • *Target Math Success* • TEC60826 • Key: inside back cover

---

Checkup 11

Name _____   Date _____

A.	$\begin{array}{r} 14 \\ -\ 8 \\ \hline \end{array}$	$\begin{array}{r} 15 \\ -\ 7 \\ \hline \end{array}$	$\begin{array}{r} 13 \\ -\ 9 \\ \hline \end{array}$	$\begin{array}{r} 16 \\ -\ 8 \\ \hline \end{array}$	$\begin{array}{r} 13 \\ -\ 5 \\ \hline \end{array}$
B.	$\begin{array}{r} 17 \\ -\ 9 \\ \hline \end{array}$	$\begin{array}{r} 13 \\ -\ 6 \\ \hline \end{array}$	$\begin{array}{r} 15 \\ -\ 8 \\ \hline \end{array}$	$\begin{array}{r} 13 \\ -\ 8 \\ \hline \end{array}$	$\begin{array}{r} 16 \\ -\ 9 \\ \hline \end{array}$
C.	$\begin{array}{r} 14 \\ -\ 9 \\ \hline \end{array}$	$\begin{array}{r} 15 \\ -\ 6 \\ \hline \end{array}$	$\begin{array}{r} 13 \\ -\ 7 \\ \hline \end{array}$	$\begin{array}{r} 17 \\ -\ 8 \\ \hline \end{array}$	$\begin{array}{r} 14 \\ -\ 6 \\ \hline \end{array}$
D.	$\begin{array}{r} 16 \\ -\ 7 \\ \hline \end{array}$	$\begin{array}{r} 15 \\ -\ 9 \\ \hline \end{array}$	$\begin{array}{r} 13 \\ -\ 4 \\ \hline \end{array}$	$\begin{array}{r} 12 \\ -\ 9 \\ \hline \end{array}$	$\begin{array}{r} 12 \\ -\ 4 \\ \hline \end{array}$
E.	$\begin{array}{r} 14 \\ -\ 5 \\ \hline \end{array}$	$\begin{array}{r} 12 \\ -\ 3 \\ \hline \end{array}$	$\begin{array}{r} 12 \\ -\ 6 \\ \hline \end{array}$	$\begin{array}{r} 14 \\ -\ 7 \\ \hline \end{array}$	$\begin{array}{r} 18 \\ -\ 9 \\ \hline \end{array}$

Test B: Subtraction facts to 18

©The Education Center, Inc. • *Target Math Success* • TEC60826 • Key: inside back cover

It's a fact!

_____

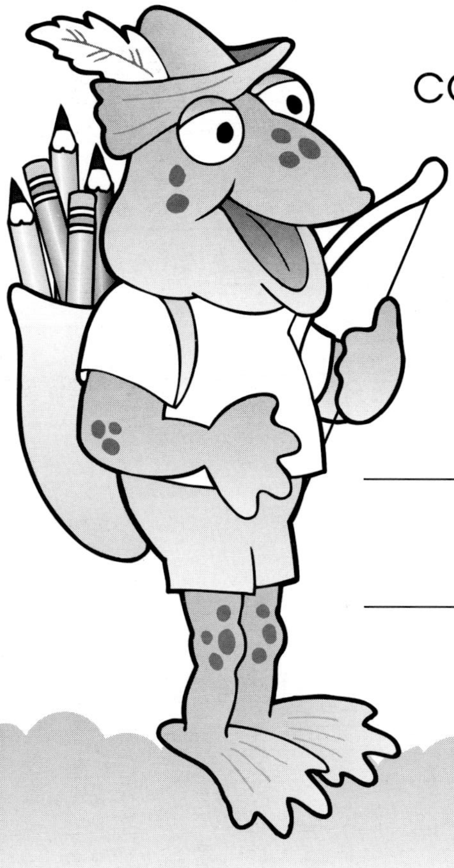

can subtract!

Teacher _____

Date _____

Congratulations!

_____

You're right
on target
with subtraction!

Teacher _____

Date _____

Home Run Hitters

Name _____ Date _____

Count.
Subtract.
Write the math sentence.

Home	Visitors
5	4

4 − 3 = 1   3 − 2 = 1

5 − 2 = 3   5 − 4 = 1

2 − 1 = 1   4 − 2 = 2

Doctor on Call

Name _____ Date _____

Subtract.
Help Dr. Ducky find his bag.
If the answer is **3**, **4**, or **5**, color the clipboard **brown**.

3 − 3 = 0   5 − 4 = 1   4 − 2 = 2   5 − 1 = 4

2 − 1 = 1   4 − 0 = 4   5 − 2 = 3   5 − 0 = 5

3 − 0 = 3   4 − 1 = 3   3 − 2 = 1   2 − 2 = 0

5 − 3 = 2   1 − 0 = 1   1 − 1 = 0   4 − 0 = 4

4 − 1 = 3   5 − 2 = 3   5 − 0 = 5   3 − 0 = 3

Beach Bound

Name _____ Date _____

Subtract.
Color by the code.

Color Code
0—orange   3—blue
1—green   4—yellow
2—red   5—purple

5 − 1 = 4   3 − 3 = 0

4 − 2 = 2   5 − 2 = 3

5 − 4 = 1   6 − 1 = 5

5 − 0 = 5   6 − 2 = 4

3 − 2 = 1   6 − 3 = 3

6 − 6 = 0   6 − 4 = 2

6 − 5 = 1   5 − 5 = 0

5 − 3 = 2   4 − 0 = 4

4 − 1 = 3   6 − 1 = 5

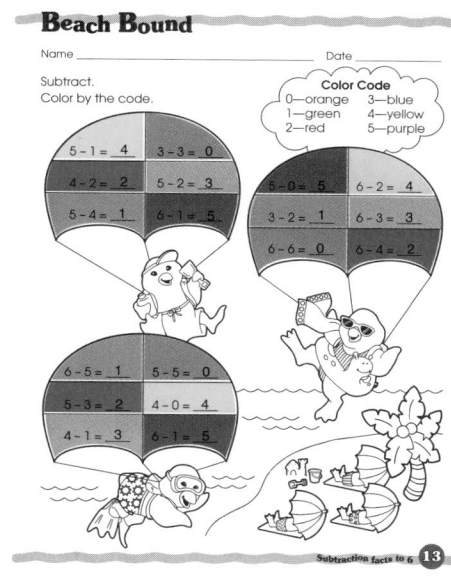

Camel's Candy Shop

Name _____ Date _____

Count.
Subtract.
Write the math sentence.

3 − 2 = 1   5 − 3 = 2

4 − 2 = 2   4 − 1 = 3

2 − 1 = 1   5 − 5 = 0

3 − 2 = 1   4 − 3 = 1

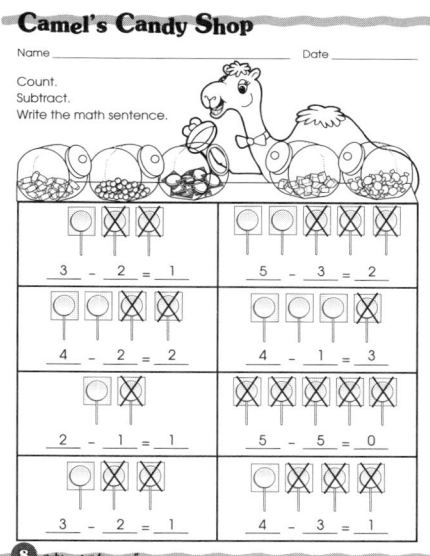

Golfin' Dolphins

Name _____ Date _____

Count.
Subtract.
Write the math sentence.

5 − 2 = 3   3 − 2 = 1

5 − 3 = 2   6 − 3 = 3

6 − 4 = 2   5 − 1 = 4

5 − 4 = 1   6 − 1 = 5

Off to School

Name _____ Date _____

Subtract.
Help Freddie Fish find his way to school.
If the answer is **1**, **2**, or **3**, color the bubble **blue**.

4 − 0 = 4   6 − 1 = 5   2 − 0 = 2   5 − 2 = 3

4 − 4 = 0   5 − 4 = 1   5 − 0 = 5   1 − 1 = 0

5 − 5 = 0   5 − 3 = 2   6 − 0 = 6   3 − 3 = 0

6 − 3 = 3   6 − 2 = 4   6 − 2 = 4

4 − 0 = 4   4 − 1 = 3

6 − 4 = 2   4 − 2 = 2

6 − 1 = 5

Fish School

Road Crew

Name _____ Date _____

Subtract.
Color by the code.

Color Code
0 or 1—orange
2 or 3—yellow
4 or 5—red

Road Crew

5 − 0 = 5   4 − 1 = 3   3 − 2 = 1   4 − 0 = 4

3 − 1 = 2   2 − 2 = 0   4 − 2 = 2   4 − 3 = 1

2 − 1 = 1   3 − 0 = 3   5 − 1 = 4   5 − 2 = 3

5 − 3 = 2   5 − 5 = 0   2 − 0 = 2   5 − 4 = 1

Cookie Countdown

Name _____ Date _____

Count.
Cross off cookies to subtract.
Write the answer.

6 − 5 = 1

5 − 1 = 4

5 − 3 = 2

4 − 2 = 2

3 − 1 = 2

2 − 1 = 1

6 − 3 = 3

4 − 3 = 1

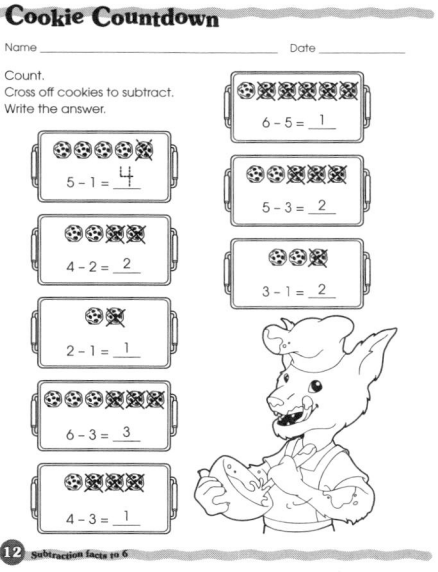

Family Photos

Name _____ Date _____

Add and subtract.

4 − 1 = 3   6 − 3 = 3   6 − 5 = 1
3 + 1 = 4   3 + 3 = 6   5 + 1 = 6
4 − 3 = 1   6 − 1 = 5
1 + 3 = 4   4 − 2 = 2   1 + 5 = 6
                2 + 2 = 4

7 − 1 = 6   7 − 5 = 2
1 + 6 = 7   2 − 1 = 1   5 + 2 = 7
7 − 6 = 1   1 + 1 = 2   7 − 2 = 5
6 + 1 = 7   2 + 5 = 7

Wow!   Oh my!

Family "Buzz-ness"

Add and subtract.
Write the numbers for each fact family on the flowers.

5 2 3
5 − 2 = 3
2 + 3 = 5
5 − 3 = 2
3 + 2 = 5

3 2 1
3 − 2 = 1
1 + 2 = 3
3 − 1 = 2
2 + 1 = 3

6 2 4
6 − 2 = 4
2 + 4 = 6
6 − 4 = 2
4 + 2 = 6

5 1 4
5 − 1 = 4
1 + 4 = 5
5 − 4 = 1
4 + 1 = 5

16 Fact families

Munch, Munch

Subtract.
Color by the code.

Color Code
0, 1, or 2—brown   3—green
4—orange   5, 6, or 7—blue

7 − 2 = 5
6 − 0 = 6
6 − 1 = 5
7 − 1 = 6
5 − 1 = 4
7 − 0 = 7
6 − 2 = 4
7 − 3 = 4
6 − 4 = 2
4 − 0 = 4
7 − 7 = 0
7 − 6 = 1
4 − 4 = 0
3 − 1 = 2
7 − 3 = 4
6 − 5 = 1
5 − 4 = 1
4 − 2 = 2
3 − 3 = 0
5 − 5 = 0
6 − 3 = 3
7 − 4 = 3

19 Subtraction facts to 7

Piggy Painting

Read each big number.
Circle **4** ways to make that number.

4
7 − 3
8 − 2
7 − 5
5 − 1
8 − 4
5 − 3

2
7 − 1
4 − 2
8 − 6
6 − 2
4 − 1
5 − 3

3
7 − 4
8 − 8
8 − 5
8 − 5
4 − 0
4 − 1

5
8 − 3
6 − 1
3 − 3
5 − 0
2 − 1
7 − 2

22 Subtraction facts to 8

Monkeying Around With Marbles

Subtract.
Cross off a
matching answer.

6 − 3 = 3   5 − 1 = 4   6 − 2 = 4   6 − 1 = 5   3 − 2 = 1

4 − 3 = 1   7 − 0 = 7   7 − 1 = 6   5 − 3 = 2   7 − 5 = 2

7 − 2 = 5   6 − 5 = 1   7 − 3 = 4

4 − 2 = 2   6 − 0 = 6   7 − 4 = 3

Answers
XXXXXXXXXXX

17 Subtraction facts to 7

Time for Bed

Subtract.
Help Eddie find his toothbrush.
If the answer is **5, 6,** or **7,**
color the box **green.**

5−3=2	7−2=5	6−1=5	7−0=7	5−4=1
4−2=2	6−0=6	3−1=2	3−0=3	2−2=0
1−1=0	5−0=5	7−1=6	6−1=5	7−6=1
7−3=4	6−4=2	5−5=0	7−0=7	6−5=1
6−0=6	7−1=6	5−0=5	7−2=5	7−4=3

20 Subtraction facts to 7

Gone Fishin'

Subtract.
Color by the code.

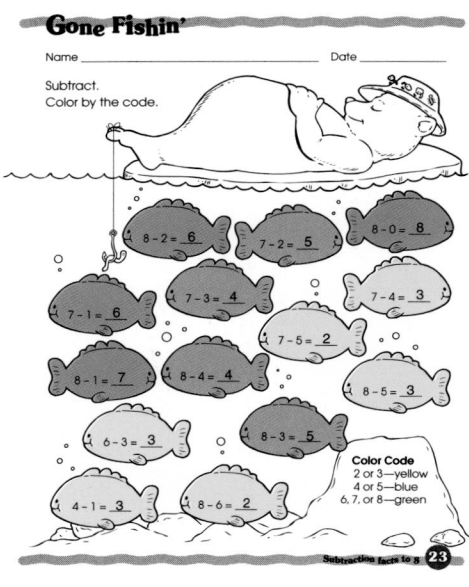

8 − 2 = 6
7 − 2 = 5
8 − 0 = 8
7 − 3 = 4
7 − 4 = 3
7 − 1 = 6
7 − 5 = 2
8 − 1 = 7
8 − 4 = 4
8 − 5 = 3
6 − 3 = 6
8 − 3 = 5
4 − 1 = 3
8 − 6 = 2

Color Code
2 or 3—yellow
4 or 5—blue
6, 7, or 8—green

23 Subtraction facts to 8

Cheep, Cheep!

Subtract.
Color by the code.

Color Code
1—orange   2 or 3—yellow
4—green   5—brown
6—red

6 − 0 = 6
3 − 2 = 1
7 − 5 = 2
2 − 1 = 1
6 − 1 = 5
7 − 1 = 6
4 − 1 = 3
5 − 3 = 2
6 − 4 = 2
6 − 0 = 6
6 − 2 = 4
3 − 0 = 3
6 − 3 = 3
7 − 4 = 3
7 − 3 = 4

18 Subtraction facts to 7

Yummy Carrot Patch

Read.
Write the math sentence.

Bunny plants **4** 🌱. She takes **2** 🌱 out. How many 🌱 are left?	There are **3** 🥕. Bunny eats **1** 🥕. How many 🥕 are left?
4 − 2 = 2	3 − 1 = 2
There are **5** 🪴. Bunny uses **1** 🪴. How many 🪴 are left?	The seed pack has **7** 🌱. Bunny plants **6** 🌱. How many 🌱 are left?
5 − 1 = 4	7 − 6 = 1
Bunny has **6** 🪴. Her friend uses **2** 🪴. How many 🪴 are left?	Bunny has **7** 🥕. She puts **3** 🥕 in a lunchbox. How many 🥕 are left?
6 − 2 = 4	7 − 3 = 4

21 Story problems: subtraction facts to 7

Hopping Home

Subtract.
Help Frog find his home.
If the answer is **4, 5,** or **6,** color the lily pad **green.**

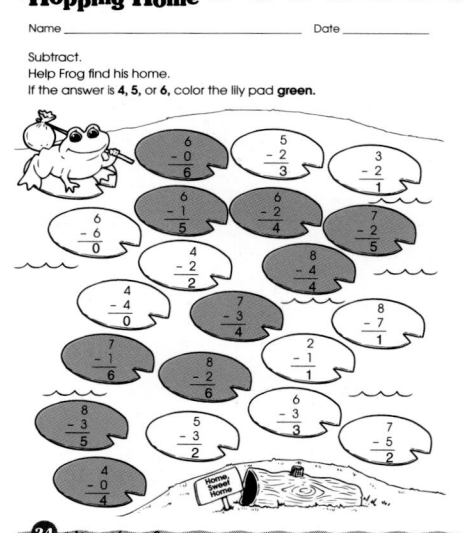

6 − 0 = 6
5 − 2 = 3
3 − 2 = 1
6 − 1 = 5
6 − 2 = 4
7 − 2 = 5
6 − 0 = 6
4 − 4 = 4
4 − 0 = 4
7 − 3 = 4
8 − 7 = 1
7 − 1 = 6
8 − 2 = 6
2 − 1 = 1
6 − 3 = 3
8 − 3 = 5
5 − 2 = 3
7 − 3 = 4
4 − 0 = 4

24 Subtraction facts to 8

Up and Over

Name _____ Date _____

Subtract.
Color by the code.

Color Code
4—brown 5—orange 6—yellow
All other answers—blue

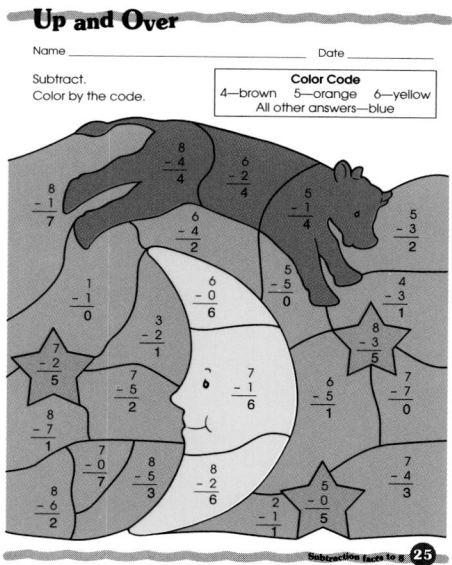

In Bloom

Name _____ Date _____

Subtract.
Color by the code.

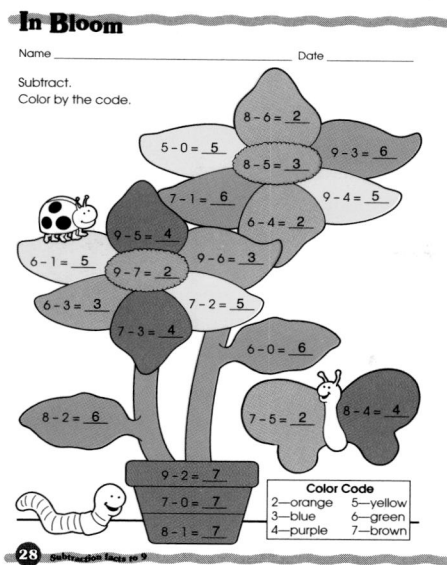

Color Code
2—orange 5—yellow
3—blue 6—green
4—purple 7—brown

Feathered Friend

Name _____ Date _____

Subtract.
Color by the code.

Color Code
5—red 7—black 9—yellow
6—orange 8—green All other answers—blue

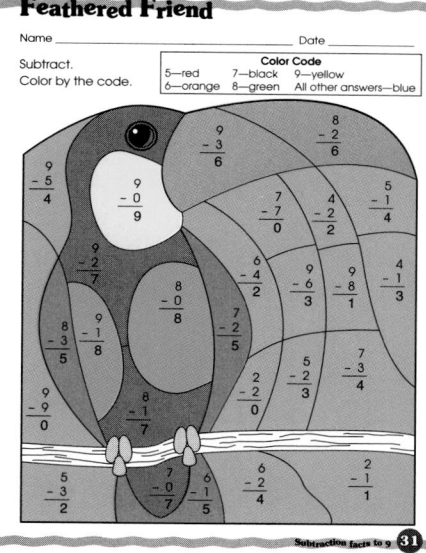

The Spider Fact Family

Name _____ Date _____

Add and subtract.

4 + 3 = 7
7 - 4 = 3
3 + 4 = 7
7 - 3 = 4

6 + 2 = 8
8 - 2 = 6
2 + 6 = 8
8 - 6 = 2

2 + 5 = 7
7 - 2 = 5
5 + 2 = 7
7 - 5 = 2

2 + 4 = 6
6 - 4 = 2
4 + 2 = 6
6 - 2 = 4

5 + 3 = 8
8 - 3 = 5
3 + 5 = 8
8 - 5 = 3

A Wild Ride

Name _____ Date _____

Subtract.
Color by the code.

Woo hoo!

1 - 0 = 1
7 - 6 = 1
9 - 5 = 4
6 - 2 = 4
9 - 2 = 7
8 - 1 = 7
5 - 3 = 2
9 - 7 = 2
7 - 2 = 5
9 - 4 = 5
6 - 3 = 3

8 - 5 = 3
4 - 1 = 3
8 - 3 = 5
5 - 0 = 5
9 - 3 = 6
7 - 1 = 6
8 - 4 = 4
4 - 0 = 4
9 - 1 = 8
3 - 1 = 2
8 - 6 = 2

Color Code
1 or 2—yellow
3 or 4—blue
5 or 6—green
7 or 8—red

Super Shoppers

Name _____ Date _____

Read.
Write the math sentence.

Frozen Foods	
He buys **8** 🍕. He eats **5** 🍕. How many are left? ___8___ - ___5___ = ___3___	She gets **9** 🍦. She mixes **3** 🍦. How many are left? ___9___ - ___3___ = ___6___
There are **9** 🥧 for sale. They buy **7** 🥧. How many are left? ___9___ - ___7___ = ___2___	She buys **8** 🍨. She eats **2** 🍨. How many are left? ___8___ - ___2___ = ___6___
He buys **9** 🍫. They eat **6** 🍫. How many are left? ___9___ - ___6___ = ___3___	There are **9** 🍧. **4** 🍧 melt. How many are left? ___9___ - ___4___ = ___5___

Birthday Surprises

Name _____ Date _____

Add and subtract.

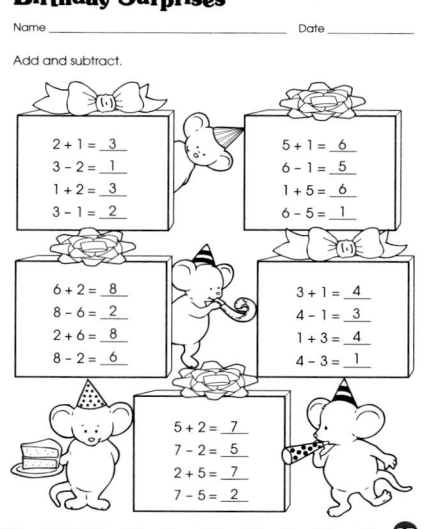

2 + 1 = 3
3 - 2 = 1
1 + 2 = 3
3 - 1 = 2

5 + 1 = 6
6 - 1 = 5
1 + 5 = 6
6 - 5 = 1

6 + 2 = 8
8 - 6 = 2
2 + 6 = 8
8 - 2 = 6

3 + 1 = 4
4 - 1 = 3
1 + 3 = 4
4 - 3 = 1

5 + 2 = 7
7 - 2 = 5
2 + 5 = 7
7 - 5 = 2

Bunches of Bubbles

Name _____ Date _____

Subtract.
Cross off a matching answer.

Answers

Where's My Melon?

Name _____ Date _____

Subtract.
Help Crow find his watermelon.
If the answer is **4** or **5**, color the melon **green**.

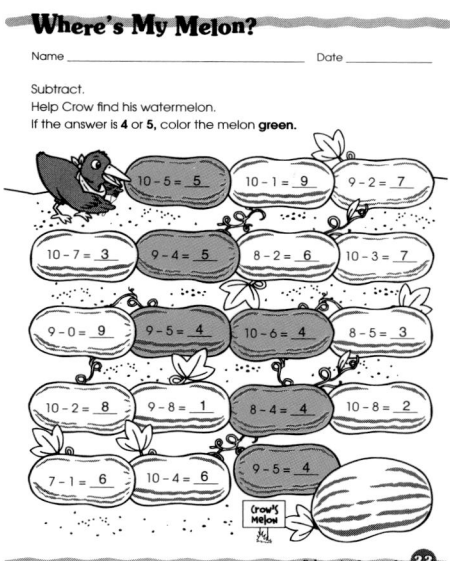

10 - 5 = 5   10 - 1 = 9   9 - 2 = 7
10 - 7 = 3   9 - 4 = 5   8 - 2 = 6   10 - 3 = 7
9 - 0 = 9   9 - 5 = 4   9 - 6 = 3
10 - 2 = 8   9 - 1 = 8   8 - 4 = 4   10 - 8 = 2
7 - 1 = 6   10 - 4 = 6   9 - 5 = 4

Crow's Melon

Just the Right Spot

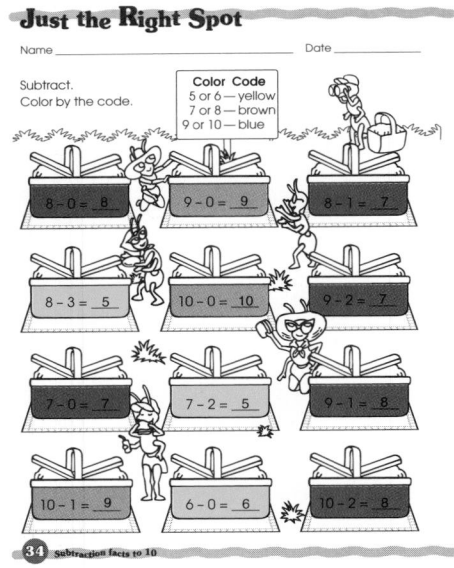

Name _____ Date _____

Subtract.
Color by the code.

Color Code
5 or 6 — yellow
7 or 8 — brown
9 or 10 — blue

8 - 0 = 8
9 - 0 = 9
8 - 1 = 7
8 - 3 = 5
10 - 0 = 10
9 - 2 = 7
7 - 0 = 7
7 - 2 = 5
9 - 1 = 8
10 - 1 = 9
6 - 0 = 6
10 - 2 = 8

34 Subtraction facts to 10

Favorite Flavors

Name _____ Date _____

Add and subtract.

Captain Sharkey's
SEASIDE ICE-CREAM SHACK

Menu
• Mackerel Fudge
• Bubble Churn
• Sardine Chip
• Octopustacio
• Squid Ripple

10 - 1 = 9
9 + 1 = 10
10 - 9 = 1
1 + 9 = 10

8 - 2 = 6
6 + 2 = 8
8 - 6 = 2
2 + 6 = 8

7 - 4 = 3
3 + 4 = 7
7 - 3 = 4
4 + 3 = 7

9 - 6 = 3
3 + 6 = 9
9 - 3 = 6
6 + 3 = 9

9 - 7 = 2
7 + 2 = 9
9 - 2 = 7
2 + 7 = 9

10 - 2 = 8
8 + 2 = 10
10 - 8 = 2
2 + 8 = 10

Fact families 37

Rrready to Go!

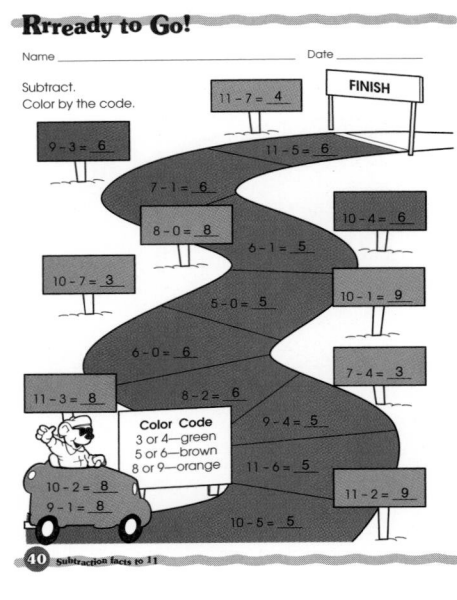

Name _____ Date _____

Subtract.
Color by the code.

11 - 7 = 4   FINISH
9 - 3 = 6
11 - 5 = 6
7 - 1 = 6
8 - 0 = 8
10 - 4 = 6
6 - 1 = 5
10 - 7 = 3
5 - 0 = 5
10 - 1 = 9
6 - 0 = 6
11 - 3 = 8
8 - 2 = 6
7 - 4 = 3

Color Code
3 or 4—green
5 or 6—brown
8 or 9—orange

9 - 4 = 5
11 - 6 = 5
9 - 1 = 8
11 - 2 = 9
10 - 5 = 5

40 Subtraction facts to 11

A Rich Fish

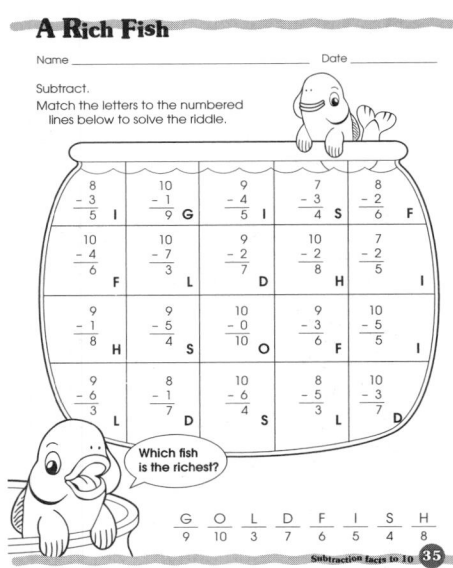

Name _____ Date _____

Subtract.
Match the letters to the numbered lines below to solve the riddle.

8 − 3 = 5	10 − 1 = 9	9 − 4 = 5	7 − 3 = 4	8 − 2 = 6
I	G	I	S	F
10 − 4 = 6	10 − 7 = 3	9 − 2 = 7	10 − 2 = 8	7 − 2 = 5
F	L	D	H	I
9 − 1 = 8	9 − 5 = 4	10 − 0 = 10	9 − 3 = 6	10 − 5 = 5
H	S	O	F	I
9 − 6 = 3	8 − 1 = 7	10 − 6 = 4	8 − 5 = 3	10 − 7 = 3
L	D	S	L	D

Which fish is the richest?

G O L D F I S H
9 10 3 7 6 5 4 8

Subtraction facts to 10 35

Wise With Numbers

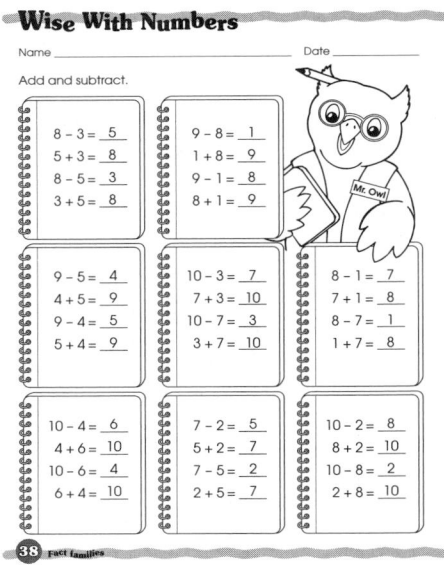

Name _____ Date _____

Add and subtract.

8 - 3 = 5
5 + 3 = 8
8 - 5 = 3
3 + 5 = 8

9 - 8 = 1
1 + 8 = 9
9 - 1 = 8
8 + 1 = 9

9 - 5 = 4
4 + 5 = 9
9 - 4 = 5
5 + 4 = 9

10 - 3 = 7
7 + 3 = 10
10 - 7 = 3
3 + 7 = 10

8 - 1 = 7
7 + 1 = 8
8 - 7 = 1
1 + 7 = 8

10 - 4 = 6
4 + 6 = 10
10 - 6 = 4
6 + 4 = 10

7 - 2 = 5
5 + 2 = 7
7 - 5 = 2
2 + 5 = 7

10 - 2 = 8
8 + 2 = 10
10 - 8 = 2
2 + 8 = 10

38 Fact families

Apple-Picking Time

Name _____ Date _____

Subtract.
Color by the code.

10 − 0 = 10
9 − 0 = 9
11 − 2 = 9
10 − 2 = 8
8 − 5 = 3
9 − 3 = 6
10 − 1 = 9
11 − 8 = 3
9 − 2 = 7

10 − 4 = 6
10 − 6 = 4
11 − 7 = 4
11 − 4 = 7
10 − 6 = 4

Color Code
3 or 4 —green
5 or 6 —brown
7 or 8 —red
9 or 10 —yellow

Subtraction facts to 11 41

Smile!

Name _____ Date _____

Subtract.
Color by the code.

How many teeth does an adult human have?

Color Code
5 or 6—purple
7—yellow

32

36 Subtraction facts to 10

Sunken Treasure

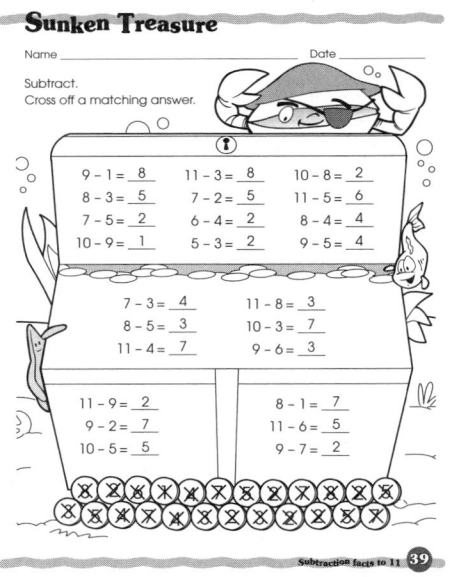

Name _____ Date _____

Subtract.
Cross off a matching answer.

9 - 1 = 8
11 - 3 = 8
10 - 8 = 2
8 - 3 = 5
7 - 2 = 5
11 - 5 = 6
7 - 5 = 2
6 - 4 = 2
8 - 4 = 4
10 - 9 = 1
5 - 3 = 2
11 - 7 = 4

7 - 3 = 4
11 - 8 = 3
8 - 5 = 3
10 - 3 = 7
11 - 4 = 7
9 - 6 = 3

11 - 9 = 2
8 - 1 = 7
9 - 2 = 7
11 - 6 = 5
10 - 5 = 5
9 - 7 = 2

Subtraction facts to 11 39

Off to the Clubhouse

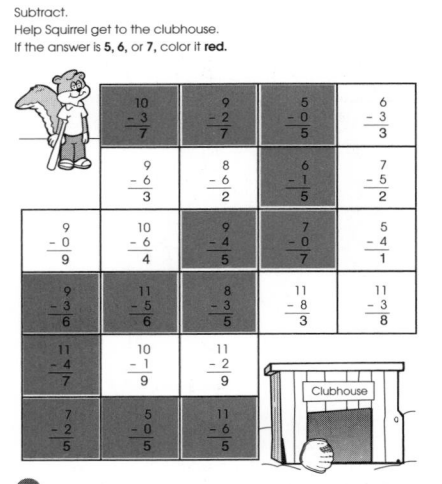

Name _____ Date _____

Subtract.
Help Squirrel get to the clubhouse.
If the answer is 5, 6, or 7, color it red.

10 − 3 = 7	9 − 2 = 7	5 − 0 = 5	6 − 3 = 3
9 − 6 = 3	8 − 6 = 2	6 − 1 = 5	7 − 5 = 2
9 − 0 = 9	10 − 6 = 4	9 − 4 = 5	7 − 0 = 7	5 − 4 = 1
9 − 3 = 6	11 − 5 = 6	8 − 3 = 5	11 − 8 = 3	11 − 3 = 8
11 − 4 = 7	10 − 1 = 9	11 − 2 = 9	
7 − 2 = 5	5 − 0 = 5	11 − 6 = 5	Clubhouse

42 Subtraction facts to 11

It's a Cookout!

Name _____ Date _____

Read.
Write the math sentence.

There are 6 burgers.
1 does not have cheese.
How many burgers have cheese?

$6 - 1 = 5$

11 burgers have pickles.
Ollie eats 3.
How many burgers are left?

$11 - 3 = 8$

There are 10 friends.
7 go home.
How many friends are left?

$10 - 7 = 3$

Ollie cooks 9 burgers.
His friends eat 7.
How many burgers are left?

$9 - 7 = 2$

Ollie cooks 11 burgers.
He burns 6.
How many burgers are left?

$11 - 6 = 5$

There are 8 burgers.
4 fall on the ground.
How many burgers are left?

$8 - 4 = 4$

Story problems: subtraction facts to 11 **43**

Animals Aloft

Name _____ Date _____

Subtract.
Color by the code.

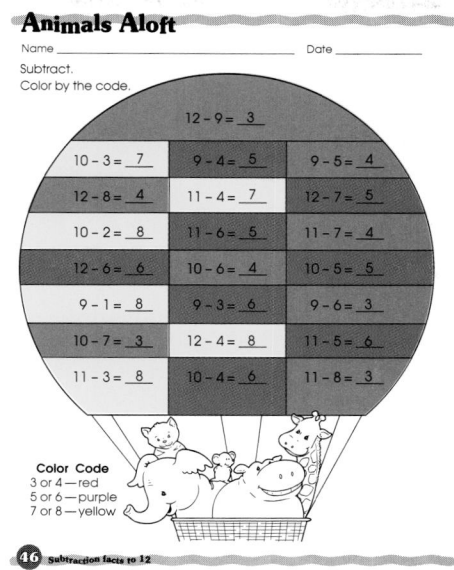

	$12 - 9 = 3$	
$10 - 3 = 7$	$9 - 4 = 5$	$9 - 5 = 4$
$12 - 8 = 4$	$11 - 4 = 7$	$12 - 7 = 5$
$10 - 2 = 8$	$11 - 6 = 5$	$11 - 7 = 4$
$12 - 6 = 6$	$10 - 6 = 4$	$10 - 5 = 5$
$9 - 1 = 8$	$9 - 3 = 6$	$9 - 6 = 3$
$10 - 7 = 3$	$12 - 4 = 8$	$11 - 5 = 6$
$11 - 3 = 8$	$10 - 4 = 6$	$11 - 8 = 3$

Color Code
3 or 4 — red
5 or 6 — purple
7 or 8 — yellow

Subtraction facts to 12 **46**

Windy Facts

Name _____ Date _____

Add and subtract.

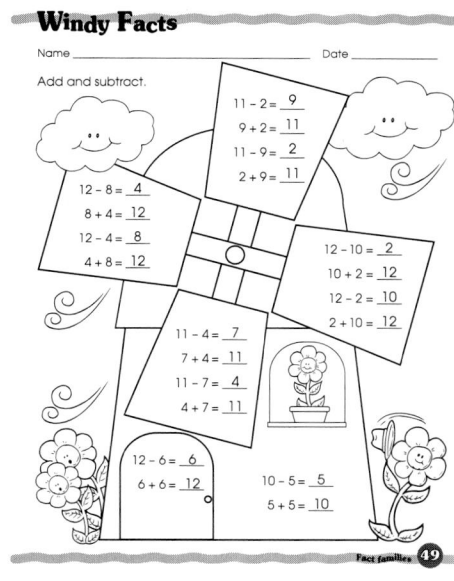

$11 - 2 = 9$
$9 + 2 = 11$
$11 - 9 = 2$
$2 + 9 = 11$

$12 - 8 = 4$
$8 + 4 = 12$
$12 - 4 = 8$
$4 + 8 = 12$

$12 - 10 = 2$
$10 + 2 = 12$
$12 - 2 = 10$
$2 + 10 = 12$

$11 - 4 = 7$
$7 + 4 = 11$
$11 - 7 = 4$
$4 + 7 = 11$

$12 - 6 = 6$
$6 + 6 = 12$

$10 - 5 = 5$
$5 + 5 = 10$

Fact families **49**

Yum! Sweet Treats

Name _____ Date _____

Read.
Write the math sentence.

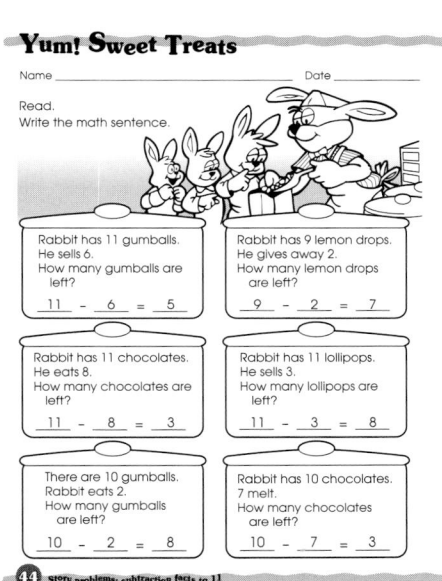

Rabbit has 11 gumballs.
He sells 6.
How many gumballs are left?

$11 - 6 = 5$

Rabbit has 9 lemon drops.
He gives away 2.
How many lemon drops are left?

$9 - 2 = 7$

Rabbit has 11 chocolates.
He eats 8.
How many chocolates are left?

$11 - 8 = 3$

Rabbit has 11 lollipops.
He sells 3.
How many lollipops are left?

$11 - 3 = 8$

There are 10 gumballs.
Rabbit eats 2.
How many gumballs are left?

$10 - 2 = 8$

Rabbit has 10 chocolates.
7 melt.
How many chocolates are left?

$10 - 7 = 3$

44 Story problems: subtraction facts to 11

Crown Prince

Name _____ Date _____

Subtract.
Color a matching answer.

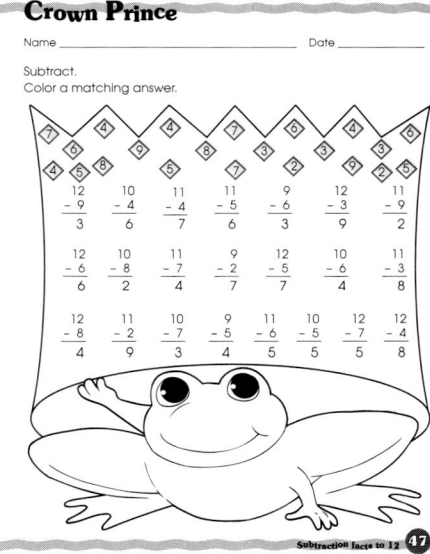

12 − 9 = 3	10 − 4 = 6	11 − 4 = 7	11 − 5 = 6	9 − 6 = 3	12 − 3 = 9	11 − 9 = 2
12 − 6 = 6	10 − 8 = 2	11 − 7 = 4	9 − 2 = 7	12 − 5 = 7	10 − 6 = 4	11 − 3 = 8
12 − 8 = 4	11 − 2 = 9	10 − 7 = 3	9 − 5 = 4	11 − 6 = 5	10 − 5 = 5	12 − 4 = 8

Subtraction facts to 12 **47**

Smooth Sailing

Name _____ Date _____

Add and subtract.

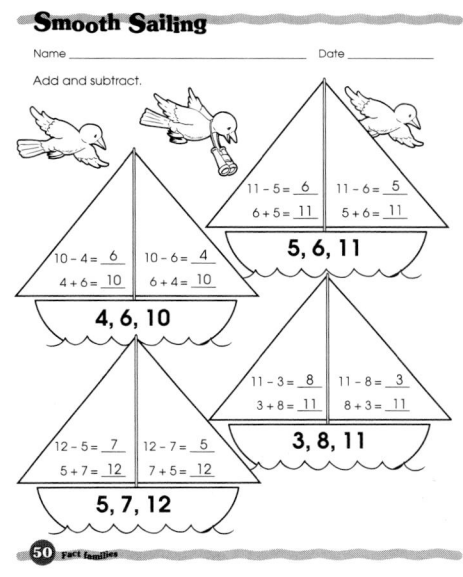

$11 - 5 = 6$
$6 + 5 = 11$

$11 - 6 = 5$
$5 + 6 = 11$

5, 6, 11

$10 - 4 = 6$
$4 + 6 = 10$

$10 - 6 = 4$
$6 + 4 = 10$

4, 6, 10

$11 - 3 = 8$
$3 + 8 = 11$

$11 - 8 = 3$
$8 + 3 = 11$

3, 8, 11

$12 - 5 = 7$
$5 + 7 = 12$

$12 - 7 = 5$
$7 + 5 = 12$

5, 7, 12

50 Fact families

Hoppin' and Poppin'

Name _____ Date _____

Look at the big number.
Circle **4** ways to make that number.

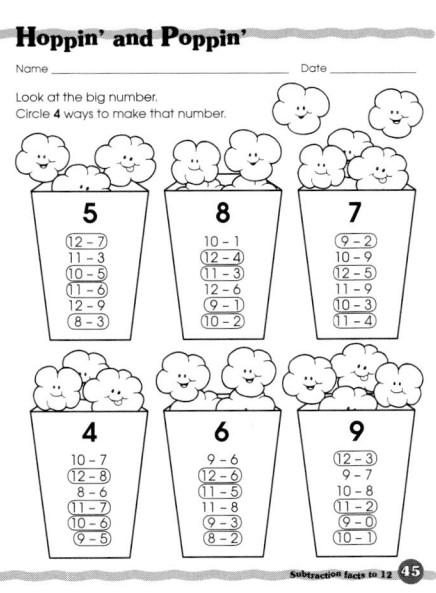

5
12 − 7
11 − 3
10 − 5
11 − 6
12 − 9
8 − 3

8
10 − 1
12 − 4
11 − 3
12 − 6
9 − 1
10 − 2

7
9 − 2
10 − 9
12 − 5
11 − 9
10 − 3
11 − 4

4
10 − 7
12 − 8
8 − 6
11 − 8
10 − 6
9 − 5

6
9 − 6
12 − 6
11 − 5
11 − 2
9 − 3
8 − 2

9
12 − 3
9 − 7
10 − 8
11 − 2
9 − 0
10 − 1

Subtraction facts to 12 **45**

Shells by the Sea

Name _____ Date _____

Subtract.
Color by the code.

$11 - 6 = 4$ $9 - 1 = 8$
$10 - 5 = 5$ $11 - 8 = 3$ $10 - 7 = 3$
$12 - 5 = 7$
$11 - 4 = 7$ $12 - 7 = 5$
$9 - 3 = 6$ $10 - 3 = 7$ $10 - 4 = 6$
$12 - 8 = 4$ $11 - 7 = 4$ $9 - 5 = 4$
$11 - 3 = 8$ $11 - 6 = 5$
$12 - 9 = 3$ $12 - 4 = 8$

Color Code
3 or 4 — blue
5 or 6 — green
7 or 8 — orange

48 Subtraction facts to 12

Top Dog!

Name _____ Date _____

Subtract.
Color by the code.

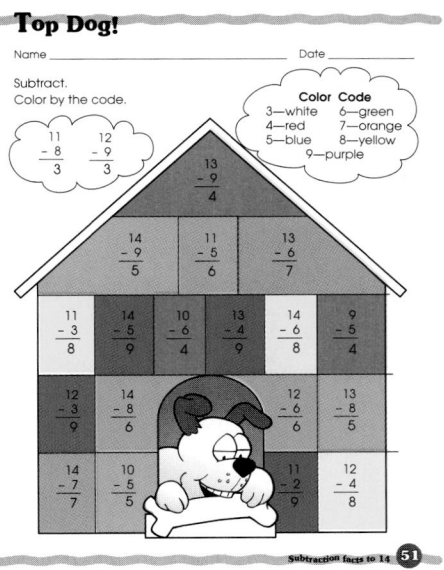

Color Code
3 — white   6 — green
4 — red   7 — orange
5 — blue   8 — yellow
             9 — purple

$11 - 8 = 3$ $12 - 9 = 3$

$13 - 9 = 4$

$14 - 9 = 5$ $11 - 5 = 6$ $13 - 6 = 7$

$11 - 3 = 8$ $14 - 5 = 9$ $10 - 6 = 4$ $13 - 5 = 8$ $14 - 6 = 8$ $9 - 5 = 4$

$11 - 3 = 8$ $14 - 8 = 6$ $12 - 6 = 6$ $13 - 8 = 5$

$14 - 7 = 7$ $10 - 5 = 5$ $11 - 2 = 9$ $12 - 4 = 8$

Subtraction facts to 14 **51**

131

A Little Monkey Business

Subtract.
Help Mr. Monkey get to his bananas.
If the answer is **5, 6,** or **7,** color it **green.**

A "Bear-y" Bright Light

Read.
Write the math sentence.

There are 12 steps.
Bear climbs 8.
How many steps are left?

$12 - 8 = 4$

There are 13 boats at sea.
6 come to the shore.
How many boats are left?

$13 - 6 = 7$

There are 13 whales.
7 swim away.
How many whales are left?

$13 - 7 = 6$

There are 14 lights.
5 burn out.
How many lights are left?

$14 - 5 = 9$

There are 14 birds.
7 fly away.
How many birds are left?

$14 - 7 = 7$

There are 12 workers.
6 go home.
How many workers are left?

$12 - 6 = 6$

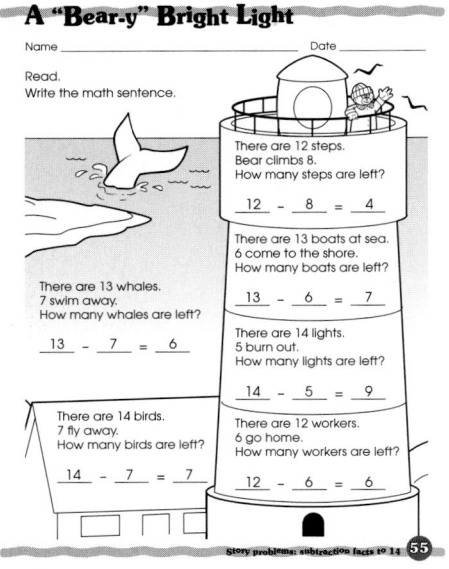

Space Sightings

Subtract.
Cross off a matching answer.

Answers

A Froggy Feast

Subtract.
If the answer is **6** or **7,** color it **green.**
Read the riddle answer.

What do frogs eat for breakfast?

Birthday Bash!

Read.
Write the math sentence.

There are 13 games.
5 are played.
How many games are left?

$13 - 5 = 8$

There are 12 balloons.
7 pop.
How many balloons are left?

$12 - 7 = 5$

There are 12 candles.
3 break.
How many candles are left?

$12 - 3 = 9$

There are 14 gifts.
8 are opened.
How many gifts are left?

$14 - 8 = 6$

There are 13 pieces of cake.
9 are eaten.
How many pieces are left?

$13 - 9 = 4$

There are 14 guests.
5 go home.
How many guests are left?

$14 - 5 = 9$

Happy Birthday!

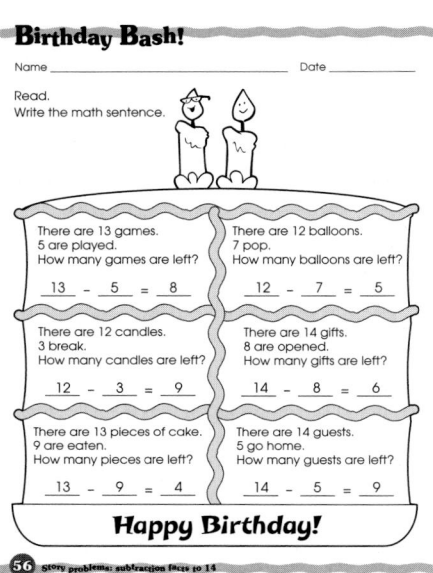

No More Honey!

Subtract.
Match the letters to the numbered
lines below to solve the riddle.

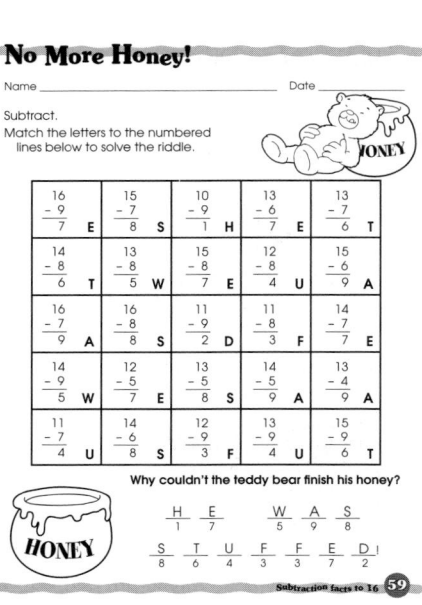

Why couldn't the teddy bear finish his honey?

H E _ _ W A S _ _
1 7   8 4 3

S T U F F E D I
8 6 4 3 3 7 2

Fishy Facts

Look at the big number.
Circle **4** ways to make
that number.

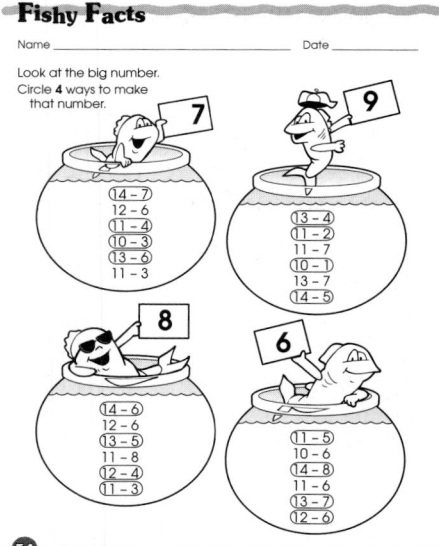

Ahoy, Matey!

Subtract.
Color by the code.

Color Code
3 or 4 — blue
5 — yellow
6 or 7 — red
8 or 9 — brown

SS Gator

Ready to Camp!

Subtract.
Help Randy Racoon find his tent.
If the answer is **6** or **7,** color the tent **yellow.**

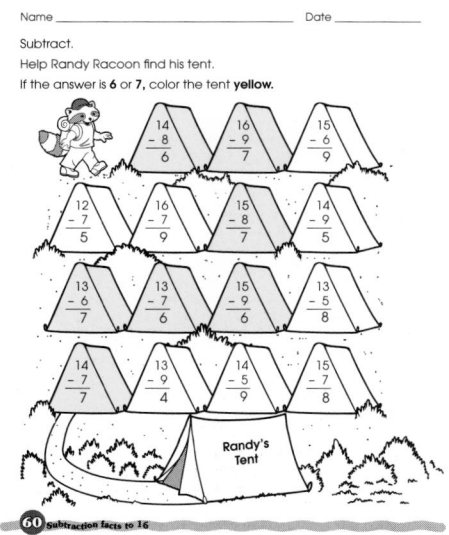

Randy's Tent

Super Scoopers

Name _____ Date _____

Add and subtract.

16 − 9 = _7_
7 + 9 = _16_
16 − 7 = _9_
9 + 7 = _16_

14 − 9 = _5_
5 + 9 = _14_
14 − 5 = _9_
9 + 5 = _14_

15 − 8 = _7_
7 + 8 = _15_
15 − 7 = _8_
8 + 7 = _15_

13 − 7 = _6_
6 + 7 = _13_
13 − 6 = _7_
7 + 6 = _13_

14 − 8 = _6_
6 + 8 = _14_
14 − 6 = _8_
8 + 6 = _14_

15 − 9 = _6_
6 + 9 = _15_
15 − 6 = _9_
9 + 6 = _15_

Fact families **61**

Hot off the Griddle!

Name _____ Date _____

Subtract.
Color by the code.

$\frac{18}{-9}{9}$ $\frac{14}{-8}{6}$ $\frac{13}{-6}{7}$ $\frac{14}{-7}{7}$ $\frac{15}{-8}{7}$ $\frac{10}{-3}{7}$ $\frac{13}{-5}{8}$ $\frac{14}{-6}{8}$

$\frac{12}{-6}{6}$ $\frac{14}{-7}{7}$ $\frac{16}{-7}{9}$ $\frac{15}{-9}{6}$ $\frac{13}{-4}{9}$ $\frac{14}{-5}{9}$ $\frac{11}{-4}{7}$ $\frac{15}{-9}{6}$

$\frac{12}{-3}{9}$ $\frac{13}{-2}{11}$ $\frac{16}{-9}{7}$ $\frac{13}{-6}{7}$ $\frac{11}{-5}{6}$ $\frac{10}{-2}{8}$ $\frac{12}{-4}{8}$ $\frac{11}{-3}{8}$

Color Code
6 or 7 — brown
8 or 9 — yellow

64 *Subtraction facts to 18*

Hey, Mom! Watch Me!

Name _____ Date _____

Read.
Write the math sentence.

17 frogs eat by the pond. 9 leave to take a nap. How many frogs are left? **17** − **9** = **8**	16 ducks swim in the pond. 7 get out. How many ducks are left? **16** − **7** = **9**
14 ducks are asleep. 8 go to play. How many ducks are left? **14** − **8** = **6**	There are 18 plants. 9 wilt. How many plants are left? **18** − **9** = **9**
There are 15 flies. A frog eats 7. How many flies are left? **15** − **7** = **8**	There are 16 lily pads. 9 float away. How many lily pads are left? **16** − **9** = **7**

Story problems: subtraction facts to 18 **67**

Barnyard Buddies

Name _____ Date _____

Add and subtract.

15 − 8 = _7_
7 + 8 = _15_
15 − 7 = _8_
8 + 7 = _15_

16 − 9 = _7_
7 + 9 = _16_
16 − 7 = _9_
9 + 7 = _16_

14 − 8 = _6_
6 + 8 = _14_
14 − 6 = _8_
8 + 6 = _14_

12 − 9 = _3_
3 + 9 = _12_
12 − 3 = _9_
9 + 3 = _12_

15 − 9 = _6_
9 + 6 = _15_
6 + 9 = _15_
15 − 6 = _9_

14 − 9 = _5_
9 + 5 = _14_
14 − 5 = _9_
5 + 9 = _14_

62 *Fact families*

Say, "Ah..."

Name _____ Date _____

Subtract.
Color by the code.

Color Code
2 or 3 — blue
4 or 5 — green
6 or 7 — orange
8 or 9 — yellow

$\frac{6}{-2}{4}$ $\frac{11}{-9}{2}$

$\frac{12}{-9}{3}$

$\frac{8}{-4}{4}$

$\frac{10}{-5}{5}$

$\frac{13}{-9}{4}$

$\frac{12}{-5}{7}$

$\frac{13}{-8}{5}$

$\frac{8}{-2}{6}$

$\frac{10}{-4}{6}$

$\frac{11}{-7}{4}$

$\frac{10}{-3}{7}$

$\frac{12}{-6}{6}$

$\frac{17}{-9}{8}$

$\frac{13}{-4}{9}$

$\frac{8}{-6}{2}$

$\frac{10}{-8}{2}$

Subtraction facts to 18 **65**

Great Teamwork!

Name _____ Date _____

Read.
Write the math sentence.

Crab has 18 shells. He buries 9. How many shells are left? **18** − **9** = **9**	There are 17 starfish. 8 go home. How many starfish are left? **17** − **8** = **9**
Octopus has 15 flags. He uses 9. How many flags are left? **15** − **9** = **6**	There are 14 pebbles on the sand castle. 6 fall off. How many pebbles are left? **14** − **6** = **8**
Starfish has 16 sticks. He loses 9. How many sticks are left? **16** − **9** = **7**	Crab finds 15 pieces of seaweed. 8 float away. How many pieces are left? **15** − **8** = **7**

68 *Story problems; subtraction facts to 18*

Round 'em Up, Cowboy!

Name _____ Date _____

Subtract.
Cross off a matching answer.

$\frac{16}{-7}{9}$ $\frac{14}{-9}{5}$ $\frac{14}{-8}{6}$ $\frac{17}{-8}{9}$ $\frac{13}{-7}{6}$ $\frac{16}{-9}{9}$

$\frac{14}{-6}{8}$ $\frac{16}{-8}{8}$ $\frac{18}{-9}{9}$ $\frac{15}{-8}{7}$ $\frac{14}{-7}{7}$ $\frac{15}{-6}{9}$

$\frac{15}{-9}{6}$ $\frac{14}{-5}{9}$ $\frac{13}{-8}{5}$ $\frac{13}{-4}{9}$ $\frac{15}{-7}{8}$ $\frac{17}{-9}{9}$

Answers
X X X X X X X
X X X X X X X
X X X X X X X

63 *Subtraction facts to 18*

Moose on the Loose

Name _____ Date _____

Subtract.
Color by the code.

$\frac{15}{-9}{6}$ $\frac{13}{-6}{7}$ $\frac{12}{-7}{5}$ $\frac{14}{-7}{7}$ $\frac{14}{-8}{6}$

$\frac{12}{-8}{4}$ $\frac{13}{-9}{4}$ $\frac{12}{-9}{3}$ $\frac{11}{-8}{3}$

$\frac{13}{-7}{6}$ $\frac{16}{-7}{9}$ $\frac{13}{-6}{7}$

$\frac{10}{-4}{6}$ $\frac{15}{-6}{9}$ $\frac{18}{-9}{9}$ $\frac{11}{-6}{5}$ $\frac{12}{-5}{7}$

$\frac{17}{-9}{8}$

$\frac{11}{-4}{7}$ $\frac{13}{-5}{8}$ $\frac{11}{-5}{6}$

$\frac{16}{-9}{7}$ $\frac{15}{-8}{7}$

Color Code
3 or 4 — yellow
5, 6, or 7 — blue   8 or 9 — brown

66 *Subtraction facts to 18*

A "Mouse-ful" of Cookies

Name _____ Date _____

Add and subtract.
Color by the code.

Color Code
1 — orange 3 — brown 5 — green
2 — yellow 4 — purple 6 — red

$\frac{4}{-2}{2}$ $\frac{5}{-2}{3}$ $\frac{6}{-4}{2}$ $\frac{2}{+3}{5}$

$\frac{1}{+1}{2}$ $\frac{1}{+3}{4}$ $\frac{3}{+1}{4}$ $\frac{5}{-4}{1}$

$\frac{3}{+3}{6}$ $\frac{2}{+1}{3}$ $\frac{1}{+3}{4}$ $\frac{3}{+3}{6}$

$\frac{6}{-5}{1}$ $\frac{1}{+7}{}$ $\frac{2}{+4}{6}$ $\frac{5}{-0}{5}$

$\frac{0}{+2}{2}$

Mixed practice to 6 **69**

133

Munching on Mixed Facts

Name _____ Date _____

Add and subtract.
Circle each answer in the picture.

5 + 1 = 6   5 − 4 = 1   2 + 1 = 3   1 + 4 = 5
4 − 2 = 2   3 + 1 = 4   4 − 4 = 0   3 + 3 = 6
6 − 3 = 3   5 − 2 = 3   4 + 2 = 6   6 − 4 = 2
3 + 2 = 5   2 + 4 = 6   6 − 5 = 1   3 − 1 = 2
0 + 3 = 3   6 − 2 = 4   3 − 3 = 0   2 + 2 = 4

72 Mixed practice to 6

To Market, to Market

Name _____ Date _____

Add and subtract.
Help Piggy get to the market.
If the answer is **4, 5,** or **6,** color the space **yellow.**

Mixed Practice to 8 75

Dinner Delivery

Name _____ Date _____

Add or subtract.
Help the ant get home.
If the answer is **4** or **5,** color it **red.**

78 Mixed practice to 10

Jungle Friends

Name _____ Date _____

Read.
Write the math sentence.

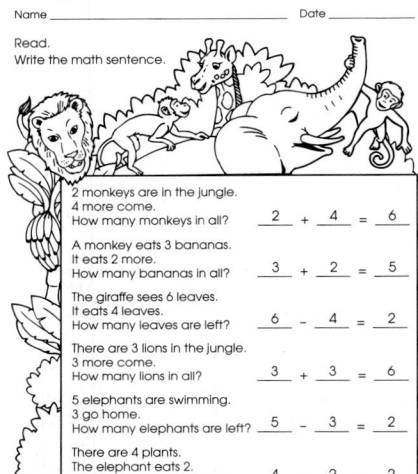

2 monkeys are in the jungle.
4 more come.
How many monkeys in all?   2 + 4 = 6

A monkey eats 3 bananas.
It eats 2 more.
How many bananas in all?   3 + 2 = 5

The giraffe sees 6 leaves.
It eats 4 leaves.
How many leaves are left?   6 − 4 = 2

There are 3 lions in the jungle.
3 more come.
How many lions in all?   3 + 3 = 6

5 elephants are swimming.
3 go home.
How many elephants are left?   5 − 3 = 2

There are 4 plants.
The elephant eats 2.
How many plants are left?   4 − 2 = 2

Story Problems: mixed practice to 6 73

Play Ball!

Name _____ Date _____

Read.
Write the math sentence.

The team has 8 bats.
2 break.
How many bats are left?   8 − 2 = 6

The pitcher chews 4 pieces of gum.
Then he chews 3 more.
How many pieces of gum in all?   4 + 3 = 7

The catcher catches 7 balls.
He drops 2.
How many balls are left?   7 − 2 = 5

Coach calls out 7 rules.
Then he calls out 1 more.
How many rules in all?   7 + 1 = 8

The player hits 5 balls.
Then he hits 3 more.
How many balls in all?   5 + 3 = 8

The team buys 8 caps.
3 get lost.
How many caps are left?   8 − 3 = 5

76 Story problems: mixed practice to 8

Al E. Gator

Name _____ Date _____

Read.
Write the math sentence.

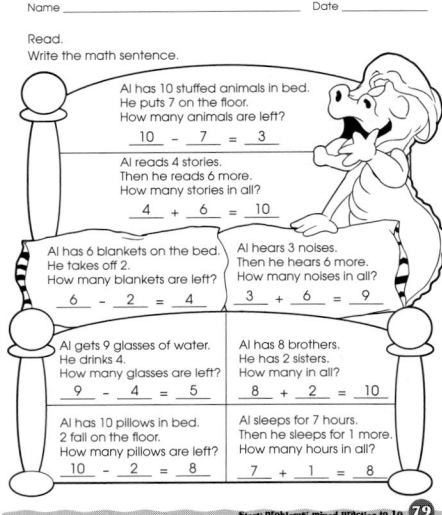

Al has 10 stuffed animals in bed.
He puts 7 on the floor.
How many animals are left?   10 − 7 = 3

Al reads 4 stories.
Then he reads 6 more.
How many stories in all?   4 + 6 = 10

Al has 6 blankets on the bed.
He takes off 2.
How many blankets are left?   6 − 2 = 4

Al hears 3 noises.
Then he hears 6 more.
How many noises in all?   3 + 6 = 9

Al gets 9 glasses of water.
He drinks 4.
How many glasses are left?   9 − 4 = 5

Al has 8 brothers.
He has 2 sisters.
How many in all?   8 + 2 = 10

Al has 10 pillows in bed.
2 fall on the floor.
How many pillows are left?   10 − 2 = 8

Al sleeps for 7 hours.
Then he sleeps for 1 more.
How many hours in all?   7 + 1 = 8

Story Problems: mixed practice to 10 79

Feeling the Rhythm

Name _____ Date _____

Add and subtract.
Color by the code.

Color Code
1 or 2—orange   3 or 4—purple
5 or 6—yellow   7 or 8—green

74 Mixed practice to 8

Dragon's Math Castle

Name _____ Date _____

Add or subtract.
Color by the code.

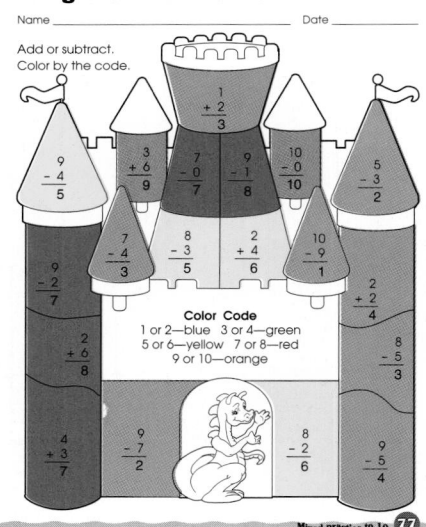

Color Code
1 or 2—blue   3 or 4—green
5 or 6—yellow   7 or 8—red
9 or 10—orange

Mixed practice to 10 77

High-Flying Facts

Name _____ Date _____

Add and subtract.
Color by the code.

Color Code
4, 5, or 6—blue
7, 8, or 9—green
10, 11, or 12—yellow

80 Mixed Practice to 12

134

Jungle Paradise

Name _____ Date _____

Add and subtract.
Cross off a matching answer.

- 3 + 9 = 12
- 12 − 4 = 8
- 6 + 5 = 11
- 5 + 7 = 12
- 11 − 2 = 9
- 12 − 6 = 6
- 11 − 9 = 2
- 12 − 5 = 7
- 4 + 8 = 12
- 12 − 9 = 3
- 5 + 6 = 11
- 11 − 10 = 1
- 11 − 7 = 4
- 11 − 4 = 7
- 12 − 7 = 5
- 9 + 3 = 12
- 11 − 6 = 5
- 7 + 5 = 12
- 12 − 8 = 4
- 4 + 6 = 10
- 11 − 3 = 8

Mixed practice to 12 **81**

Chicken Chase

Name _____ Date _____

Add and subtract.
Color a matching answer in the picture.

- 5 + 9 = 14
- 12 − 9 = 3
- 6 + 5 = 11
- 7 + 7 = 14
- 13 − 8 = 5
- 5 + 8 = 13
- 14 − 8 = 6
- 4 + 7 = 11
- 14 − 5 = 9
- 3 + 9 = 12
- 13 − 6 = 7
- 6 + 8 = 14
- 13 − 9 = 4
- 14 − 6 = 8
- 6 + 6 = 12
- 4 + 8 = 12
- 13 − 4 = 9
- 14 − 9 = 5
- 4 + 9 = 13
- 13 − 7 = 6
- 14 − 7 = 7
- 6 + 7 = 13
- 13 − 5 = 8
- 5 + 7 = 12

84 Mixed practice to 14

Made in the Shade

Name _____ Date _____

Add and subtract.
Cross off a matching answer.

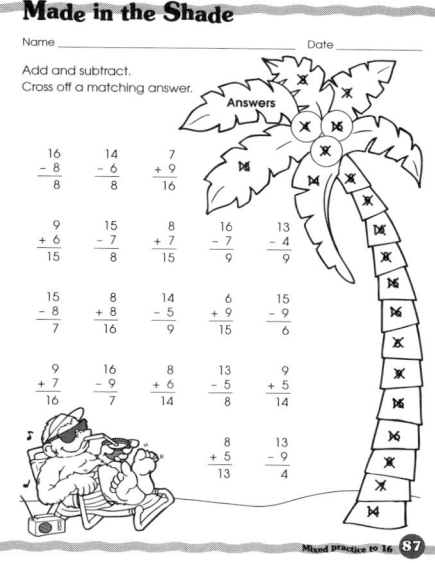

Answers

- 16 − 8 = 8
- 14 − 6 = 8
- 7 + 9 = 16
- 9 + 6 = 15
- 15 − 7 = 8
- 8 + 7 = 15
- 16 − 7 = 9
- 13 − 4 = 9
- 15 − 8 = 7
- 8 + 8 = 16
- 14 − 5 = 9
- 6 + 9 = 15
- 15 − 9 = 6
- 9 + 7 = 16
- 16 − 9 = 7
- 8 + 6 = 14
- 13 − 5 = 8
- 9 + 5 = 14
- 8 + 5 = 13
- 13 − 9 = 4

Mixed practice to 16 **87**

Pete the Pretzel Pal

Name _____ Date _____

Read.
Write the math sentence.

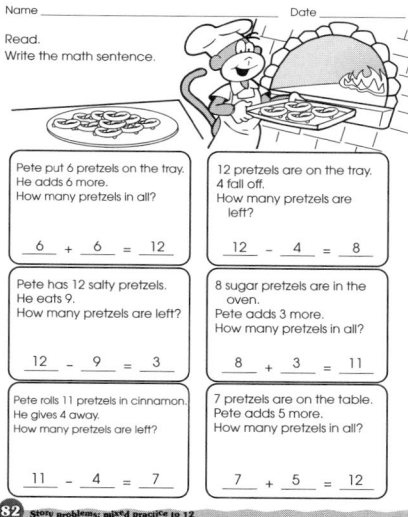

- Pete put 6 pretzels on the tray. He adds 6 more. How many pretzels in all?
  6 + 6 = 12
- 12 pretzels are on the tray. 4 fall off. How many pretzels are left?
  12 − 4 = 8
- Pete has 12 salty pretzels. He eats 9. How many pretzels are left?
  12 − 9 = 3
- 8 sugar pretzels are in the oven. Pete adds 3 more. How many pretzels in all?
  8 + 3 = 11
- Pete rolls 11 pretzels in cinnamon. He gives 4 away. How many pretzels are left?
  11 − 4 = 7
- 7 pretzels are on the table. Pete adds 5 more. How many pretzels in all?
  7 + 5 = 12

82 Story problems: mixed practice to 12

Pigs in Wigs

Name _____ Date _____

Read.
Write the math sentence.

- There are 9 long wigs. There are 4 short wigs. How many wigs are there in all?
  9 + 4 = 13
- There are 14 pigs. 2 go home. How many pigs are left?
  14 − 2 = 12
- There are 13 wigs. 2 are curly. How many wigs are not curly?
  13 − 2 = 11
- There are 6 brushes. There are 8 combs. How many are there in all?
  6 + 8 = 14
- There are 12 wigs. The pigs try on 8. How many wigs did the pigs not try on?
  12 − 8 = 4
- 7 wigs are black. 6 wigs are brown. How many wigs are there in all?
  7 + 6 = 13
- There are 8 short pigs. There are 4 tall pigs. How many pigs are there in all?
  8 + 4 = 12
- There are 13 wigs. The pigs buy 4. How many wigs are left?
  13 − 4 = 9

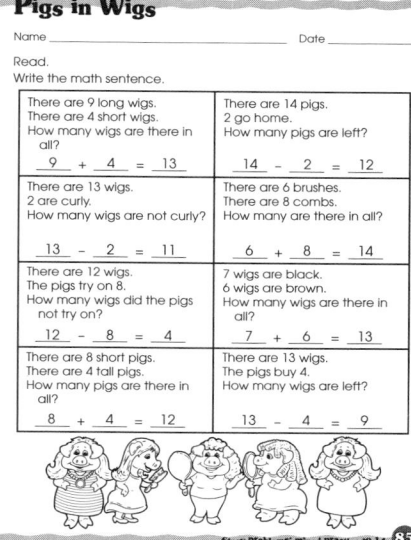

Story problems: mixed practice to 14 **85**

A "Bear-y" Fun Time!

Name _____ Date _____

Read.
Write the math sentence.

- Bear catches 16 fish. He puts 9 back in the water. How many fish are left?
  16 − 9 = 7
- 9 bears go swimming. 7 more bears go swimming. How many go swimming in all?
  9 + 7 = 16
- Bear has 6 fishing rods. He buys 9 more. How many fishing rods in all?
  6 + 9 = 15
- There are 15 headphones. Bear takes 8. How many headphones are left?
  15 − 8 = 7
- Bear reads 7 books. He reads 8 more. How many books does he read in all?
  7 + 8 = 15
- There are 14 inner tubes. 8 pop. How many inner tubes are left?
  14 − 8 = 6

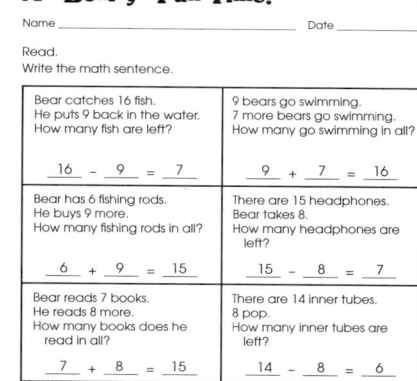

88 Story problems: mixed practice to 16

"SSSuper" Math

Name _____ Date _____

Add and subtract.
Color by the code.

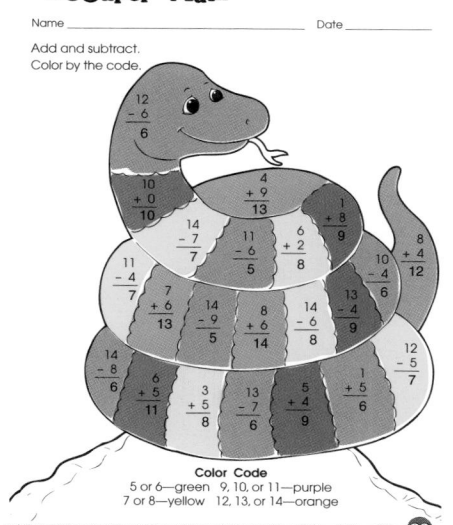

- 12 − 6 = 6
- 10 + 0 = 10
- 4 + 9 = 13
- 1 + 8 = 9
- 11 − 7 = 4
- 11 − 6 = 5
- 6 + 2 = 8
- 8 + 4 = 12
- 11 − 4 = 7
- 7 + 6 = 13
- 9 − 5 = 4
- 8 + 6 = 14
- 10 + 2 = 12
- 14 − 8 = 6
- 6 + 5 = 11
- 3 + 5 = 8
- 13 − 7 = 6
- 5 + 4 = 9
- 1 + 6 = 7
- 12 − 5 = 7

Color Code
5 or 6—green 9, 10, or 11—purple
7 or 8—yellow 12, 13, or 14—orange

Mixed practice to 14 **83**

Pretty As a Painting

Name _____ Date _____

Add and subtract.
Color by the code.

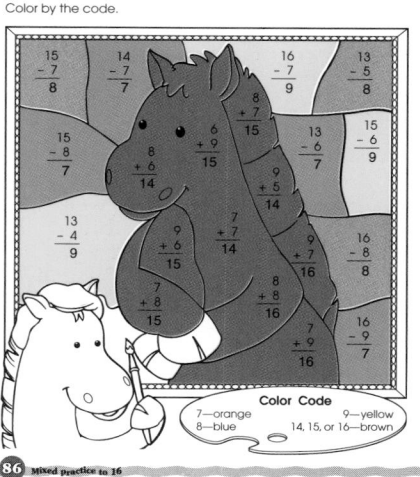

- 15 − 7 = 8
- 14 − 6 = 8
- 16 − 7 = 9
- 13 − 5 = 8
- 8 + 7 = 15
- 15 − 8 = 7
- 13 − 6 = 7
- 15 − 6 = 9
- 13 − 4 = 9
- 8 + 9 = 17
- 9 + 6 = 15
- 7 + 7 = 14
- 5 + 9 = 14
- 16 − 8 = 8
- 8 + 8 = 16
- 7 + 9 = 16
- 9 + 7 = 16
- 16 − 9 = 7

Color Code
7—orange 9—yellow
8—blue 14, 15, or 16—brown

86 Mixed practice to 16

Falling Numbers

Name _____ Date _____

Add or subtract.
Color by the code.

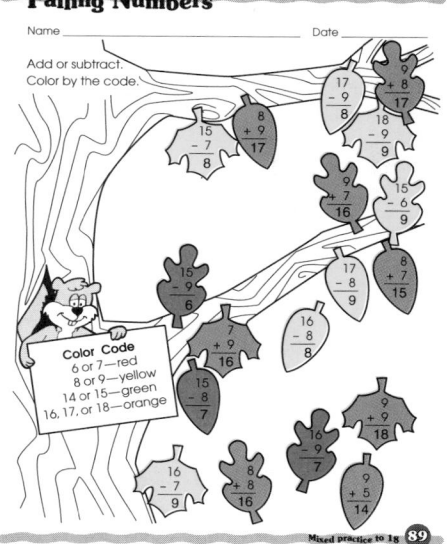

- 17 − 9 = 8
- 9 + 8 = 17
- 15 − 7 = 8
- 8 + 9 = 17
- 18 − 9 = 9
- 9 + 7 = 16
- 15 − 6 = 9
- 15 − 9 = 6
- 17 − 8 = 9
- 8 + 7 = 15
- 16 − 8 = 8
- 9 + 9 = 18
- 15 − 8 = 7
- 16 − 7 = 9
- 16 − 9 = 7
- 9 + 5 = 14

Color Code
6 or 7—red
8 or 9—yellow
14 or 15—green
16, 17, or 18—orange

Mixed practice to 18 **89**

Cool Character

Name _____ Date _____

Add or subtract.
Color by the code.

Color Code
6—white 7—red 8—black
14, 15, or 16—blue
17 or 18—yellow

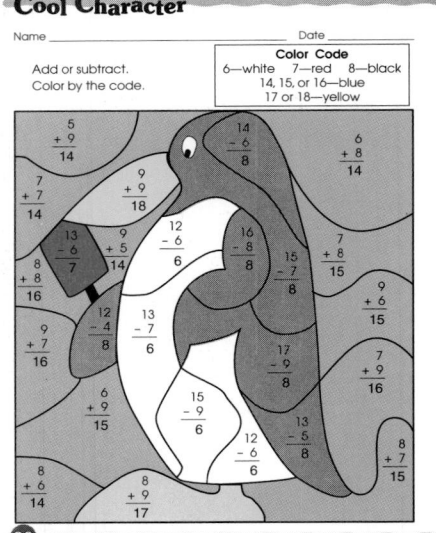

90 Mixed practice to 18

A Crunchy Carrot Crop

Name _____ Date _____

Count back 1.
Use the number line to help you.

10 - 1 = 9   6 - 1 = 5

8 - 1 = 7   2 - 1 = 1

1 - 1 = 0   7 - 1 = 6

4 - 1 = 3   5 - 1 = 4

9 - 1 = 8   3 - 1 = 2

95 Counting back 1

Nuts About Numbers

Name _____ Date _____

Subtract.
Color by the code.

Color Code
1, 2, or 3—blue 4—green 5—red
6, 7, 8, 9, or 10—brown

98 Subtracting 0

"Fix-o-saurus"

Name _____ Date _____

Dexter the dinosaur fixes cars.
Read.
Write the math sentence.

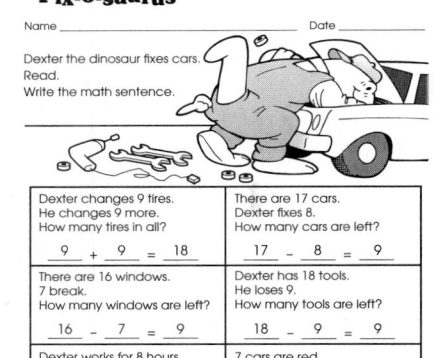

Dexter changes 9 tires. He changes 9 more. How many tires in all? 9 + 9 = 18	There are 17 cars. Dexter fixes 8. How many cars are left? 17 - 8 = 9
There are 16 windows. 7 break. How many windows are left? 16 - 7 = 9	Dexter has 18 tools. He loses 9. How many tools are left? 18 - 9 = 9
Dexter works for 8 hours. He works 9 more. How many hours in all? 8 + 9 = 17	7 cars are red. 9 cars are blue. How many cars in all? 7 + 9 = 16
There are 8 broken lights. There are 8 more lights. How many lights in all? 8 + 8 = 16	Dexter has 17 customers. 9 go home. How many customers are left? 17 - 9 = 8

91 Story Problems: mixed practice to 18

Monkeying Around the Playground

Name _____ Date _____

Count back 2.
Use the number line to help you.

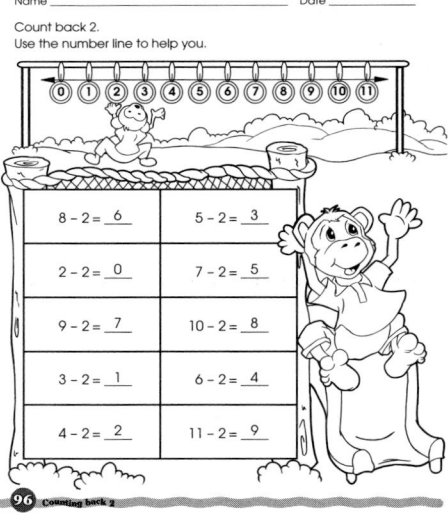

8 - 2 = 6   5 - 2 = 3

2 - 2 = 0   7 - 2 = 5

9 - 2 = 7   10 - 2 = 8

3 - 2 = 1   6 - 2 = 4

4 - 2 = 2   11 - 2 = 9

96 Counting back 2

Sweet Treat

Name _____ Date _____

Subtract.
Color.

If a number is subtracted from itself, color the space purple.

99 Subtracting a number from itself

Drive-In Dining

Name _____ Date _____

Read.
Write the math sentence.

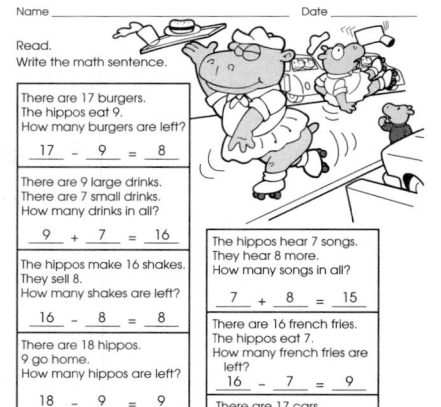

There are 17 burgers. The hippos eat 9. How many burgers are left? 17 - 9 = 8	
There are 9 large drinks. There are 7 small drinks. How many drinks in all? 9 + 7 = 16	
The hippos make 16 shakes. They sell 8. How many shakes are left? 16 - 8 = 8	The hippos hear 7 songs. They hear 8 more. How many songs in all? 7 + 8 = 15
There are 18 hippos. 9 go home. How many hippos are left? 18 - 9 = 9	There are 16 french fries. The hippos eat 7. How many french fries are left? 16 - 7 = 9
The hippos make 9 hot dogs. They make 9 more. How many hot dogs in all? 9 + 9 = 18	There are 17 cars. 8 drive away. How many cars are left? 17 - 8 = 9

92 Story problems: mixed practice to 18

An "Apple-tizing" Snack

Name _____ Date _____

Count back 3.
Use the number line to help you.

9 - 3 = 6   3 - 3 = 0

12 - 3 = 9   7 - 3 = 4

4 - 3 = 1   10 - 3 = 7

8 - 3 = 5   6 - 3 = 3

11 - 3 = 8   5 - 3 = 2

97 Counting back 3

It's Lunchtime

Name _____ Date _____

Subtract.
Add to check your answer.

4 - 1 = 3	3 + 1 = 4	6 - 2 = 4	4 + 2 = 6
8 - 3 = 5	5 + 3 = 8	9 - 4 = 5	5 + 4 = 9
7 - 6 = 1	1 + 6 = 7	9 - 6 = 3	3 + 6 = 9
10 - 1 = 9	9 + 1 = 10	3 - 2 = 1	1 + 2 = 3
5 - 3 = 2	2 + 3 = 5	8 - 6 = 2	6 + 2 = 8

100 Using addition to check subtraction

136